POITIERS AD 732

Charles Martel turns the Islamic tide

CAMPAIGN • 190

POITIERS AD 732

Charles Martel turns the Islamic tide

DAVID NICOLLE

ILLUSTRATED BY GRAHAM TURNER

Series editors Marcus Cowper and Nikolai Bogdanovic

First published in Great Britain in 2008 by Osprey Publishing,
Midland House, West Way, Botley, Oxford OX2 0PH, UK
443 Park Avenue South, New York, NY 10016, USA
E-mail: info@ospreypublishing.com

A CIP catalogue record for this book is available from the British Library.

ISBN: 978 1 84603 230 1

Editorial by Ilios Publishing Ltd, Oxford, UK (www.iliospublishing.com)
Page layout by The Black Spot
Index by Auriol Griffith-Jones
Typeset in Myriad Pro and Sabon
Maps by the Map Studio Ltd
3D bird's-eye views by The Black Spot
Battlescene illustrations by Graham Turner
Originated by United Graphic Pte Ltd., Singapore
Printed in China through World Print Ltd

08 09 10 11 12   10 9 8 7 6 5 4 3 2 1

FOR A CATALOGUE OF ALL BOOKS PUBLISHED BY OSPREY MILITARY
AND AVIATION PLEASE CONTACT:

NORTH AMERICA
Osprey Direct, c/o Random House Distribution Center, 400 Hahn Road,
Westminster, MD 21157
E-mail: info@ospreydirect.com

ALL OTHER REGIONS
Osprey Direct UK, P.O. Box 140 Wellingborough, Northants, NN8 2FA, UK
E-mail: info@ospreydirect.co.uk

www.ospreypublishing.com

DEDICATION
In memoriam Jillian Honisett, the best of neighbours

ARTIST'S NOTE

Readers may care to note that the original paintings from which the
colour plates in this book were prepared are available for private sale.
All reproduction copyright whatsoever is retained by the Publishers.
All enquiries should be addressed to:

Graham Turner
PO Box 568
Aylesbury
Buckinghamshire
HP17 8ZK, UK

The Publishers regret that they can enter into no correspondence
upon this matter.

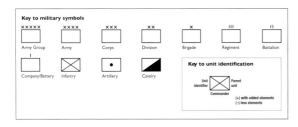

CONTENTS

The Umayyad Caliphate and its neighbours, *c.* AD 730

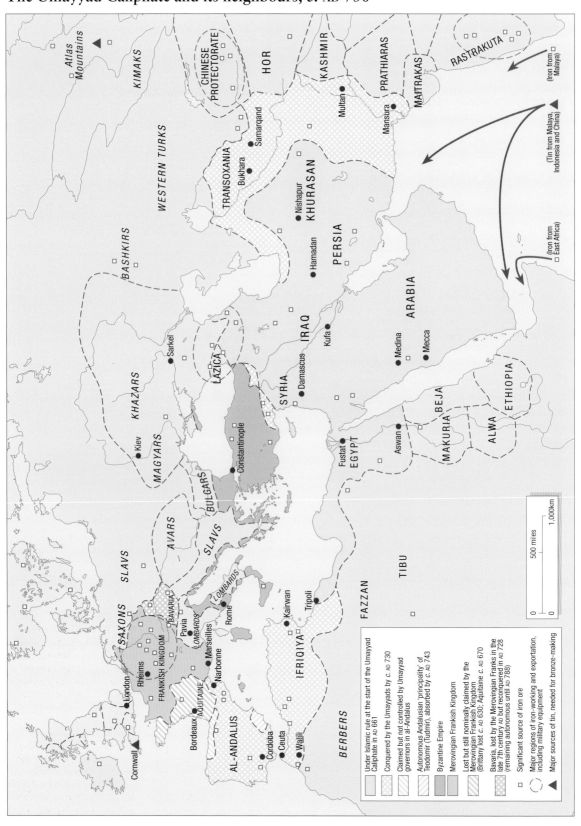

Atlas Mountains

KIMAKS

CHINESE PROTECTORATE

HOR

KASHMIR

PRATHIARAS

MAITRAKAS

RASTRAKUTA

(Iron from Malaya)

(Tin from Malaya, Indonesia and China)

Multan

Mansura

WESTERN TURKS

Samarqand

TRANSOXANIA

Bukhara

Nishapur

KHURASAN

PERSIA

(Iron from East Africa)

BASHKIRS

Hamadan

ARABIA

KHAZARS

Sarkel

LAZICA

IRAQ

Kufa

Damascus

SYRIA

Medina

Mecca

Kiev

MAGYARS

Constantinople

BULGARS

ETHIOPIA

Fustat

EGYPT

Aswan

MAKURIA

BEJA

ALWA

AVARS

SLAVS

TIBU

SAXONS

SLAVS

LOMBARDS

Rome

Pavia

BAVARIA

LOMBARDS

Kairwan

Tripoli

FAZZAN

London

Rheims

FRANKISH KINGDOM

Marseilles

Narbonne

AQUITAINE

Bordeaux

IFRIQIYA

Cornwall

AL-ANDALUS

Cordoba

Ceuta

Walili

BERBERS

500 miles

1,000km

Under Islamic rule at the start of the Umayyad Caliphate in AD 661

Conquered by the Umayyads by *c.* AD 730

Claimed but not controlled by Umayyad governors in al-Andalus

Autonomous Andalusian 'principality of Teodomir' (Tudmir), absorbed by *c.* AD 743

Byzantine Empire

Merovingian Frankish Kingdom

Lost but still nominally claimed by the Merovingian Frankish Kingdom (Brittany lost *c.* AD 630; Aquitaine *c.* AD 670)

Bavaria, lost by the Merovingian Franks in the late 7th century AD but reconquered in AD 728 (remaining autonomous until AD 788)

Significant source of iron ore

Major regions of iron-working and exportation, including military equipment

Major sources of tin, needed for bronze-making

INTRODUCTION

The battle of Poitiers was just one episode during a period of huge events, yet its description as 'the breaking of the tidal wave of Islamic expansion in Western Europe', remains essentially accurate. What is less justified is the belief that Charles Martel, the Frankish commander, somehow 'saved Western Christian civilization' from destruction.

In reality, the wave of Arab-Islamic expansion that began in the mid-7th century AD was already drawing to a halt not only in Europe but also in the Caucasus, Central Asia, India and Africa. Less than a generation later the Syrian-based Umayyad Caliphate, the first ruling dynasty in Islamic history, was overthrown by the Abbasid Caliphate based in Iraq. Similarly, the enfeebled Merovingian dynasty that had ruled the Frankish Kingdom for centuries would soon be replaced by that of the Carolingian descendants of Charles Martel, of whom Charlemagne would be the greatest. The Byzantine Empire, squeezed between the originally Germanic, supposedly 'barbarian' kingdoms of Europe and the expanding empire of Islam, was now re-emerging from a period of military disaster but was about to enter another period of instability characterized by iconoclasm, a Christian movement that frowned upon devotion to religious images. Iconoclasm would fail within Byzantium but the tensions it caused would deepen the existing religious tensions between Rome and Constantinople, Pope and Emperor, eventually resulting in the emergence of separate strands of Christianity – Roman Catholic and Orthodox.

When the Muslims overthrew the Visigothic Kingdom in the area which now forms Spain and Portugal, Toledo was its capital. They initially transferred the centre of government to Seville, in close maritime contact with North Africa, but in AD 716 the Umayyad governor moved it to Cordova where his successors built the magnificent Great Mosque, seen near the end of the Roman bridge, which the Muslims also repaired. (Author's photograph)

The allegorical figure of 'Triumph' on a 9th-century, French, carved ivory plaque. The armour might be a very stylized representation of a short-sleeved mail hauberk, while the round shield and large-bladed spear were typical Frankish equipment of this and previous centuries. (Bargello Museum, Florence; author's photograph)

The 8th century AD is often still regarded as part of a so-called Dark Age in history; a concept that is misleading even within Europe and is totally inaccurate for the emerging Islamic world, which had entered a golden age of economic expansion and cultural creativity. This having been said, the optimism that had characterized much of 6th- and early 7th-century Christendom had been replaced by a widespread sense of foreboding, many believing that the rise of Islam was associated with the impending end of the world. Attitudes were, of course, different amongst Muslims. Their huge conquests had reached from the Atlantic to almost the frontiers of China, from Central Asia to the Sudan, and had a huge economic as well as cultural impact. Trade was expanding rapidly and even the serious shortage of iron resources within the Islamic heartlands had a positive impact in that it stimulated a massive trade in raw materials, sometimes from far beyond the frontiers of the Islamic world.

THE ISLAMIC CONQUESTS AND THE UMAYYAD CALIPHATE

The expansion of Islam had been the most dramatic event of the 7th and early 8th centuries AD, and had recently incorporated both the Iberian Peninsula and Septimania, in what is now southern France. However, it is impossible to understand the Poitiers campaign of AD 732 without knowing what was happening elsewhere in the vast Umayyad Caliphate. In many respects Arab-Islamic expansion was just another movement of Semitic peoples from the Arabian Peninsula into neighbouring territories, as had been going on for millenia. There had been no attack upon Christianity as a religion and the conquest could be interpreted as a Semitic takeover that replaced the authority, if not the administration, of the previous Romano-Byzantine and Sassanian Iranian empires. Success bred success and the conquests took on a momentum of their own as the increasingly professional armies of the caliphate acquired further land and booty.

Yet almost from the very beginning there had been tension between rival Arab tribes or clans, which supposedly reflected an ancient rivalry between the 'Qays' and 'Kalb' factions, nominally 'northern' and 'southern' Arabs whose actual geographical location was often completely the opposite! Mu'awiya, the first and arguably greatest of the Umayyad caliphs (AD 661–680), had worked hard to win the support of the militarily sophisticated Syrian tribes, both those who had converted to Islam and those who had not yet done so. Although the military leadership of the Arab-Islamic campaigns as yet remained largely in the hands of 'newcomers' from the Arabian Peninsula, under Mu'awiya and his most effective Umayyad successors the elite troops of Bilad al-Sham, 'The Land of Greater Syria', included units drawn from both tribal groups, with the Syrian Kalb tribes gradually increasing in importance. Another feature of this Umayyad period was the integration of conquered peoples into Islamic society; conversion to Islam theoretically meant equality and brotherhood, especially for those who served in Muslim armies.

In specifically military terms, the excellent communications that supported the astonishing economic development of the caliphate also gave its armies a strategic advantage over most of their rivals. Economic development was also reflected in the rapid growth of arms-manufacturing centres within the Middle Eastern heartlands of the caliphate. In fact Hisham, the Umayyad

A small carving in the early 8th-century Umayyad garrison town of Anjar in Lebanon has been described as a confrontation between the Umayyad caliph and his Byzantine or Sassanian foes, or as a hunting scene. The carving is also evidence that there was no ban on representational sculpture within a secular context during the Umayyad period. (*in situ* palace area of Anjar; author's photograph)

who ruled at the time of the Poitiers campaign, was credited by the chronicler al-Mas'udi with 'perfecting the production of arms and armour'.

Though Syria was the political and military centre of the Umayyad Caliphate, there was also a considerable development in Iraq while Iran entered into a golden age. The same was true of Transoxania to the north-east, though the military potential of these huge regions had little impact upon the westernmost Islamic provinces in North Africa and the Iberian Peninsula. Nevertheless, the Umayyad state was now facing major military difficulties on its central and eastern fronts, against a revived Byzantine Empire, the formidable Turkish Khazar Khanate and the Türgesh or Western Turks.

Under such circumstances the affairs of the distant west came a poor second in the Caliph Hisham's strategic priorities, though here things seemed to be going much better. There had been no serious trouble in Egypt since a Coptic Christian uprising was crushed in AD 725 and a naval base had been established in the neighbouring Libyan province of Barqa in AD 713. A ban on major naval expeditions, imposed following a disastrous Muslim maritime campaign against Abyssinia in AD 641, had been lifted but serious naval losses during the failed Umayyad assault upon the Byzantine capital of Constantinople in AD 717 threatened the Muslims' maritime link between North Africa and the recently conquered province of al-Andalus. However, within little more than a decade Umayyad fleets were again regularly raiding Byzantine-ruled islands in the central and western Mediterranean.

AL-ANDALUS AND NORTH AFRICA

The Islamic overthrow of the seemingly powerful Germanic Visigothic Kingdom in what are now Spain and Portugal in the early 8th century AD was a major event in European history. Until then the Iberian Peninsula had been flourishing in cultural if not political or economic terms, and even the supposed decline of its ex-Roman towns is being challenged by archaeological research. Now the Umayyad governors of what Muslim sources called al-Andalus faced much the same military problems as their Visigothic predecessors; above all how to control the Basques and other pagan, or only nominally Christian, peoples of the north.

The Visigothic kingdom may also have dominated a small part of northern Morocco in the late 7th century AD, including the port of Ceuta (Sabta in Arabic), just as the Arabs were advancing from the east. The Visigothic Kingdom was similarly in close cultural and economic contact by sea with the Celtic regions of Ireland, western Britain and Brittany. Though Celtic naval power declined in the 7th century AD, this Atlantic link seems to have survived the Islamic conquest, not least because of the importance of Cornish tin, which was exported into at least the western half of the Islamic world.

Remarkably little is known about North African Berber culture and history in the immediate pre-Islamic period. Byzantine imperial control had by then been reduced to a series of coastal enclaves, except around Carthage in what is now northern Tunisia where there had even been some urban revival during the 7th century AD. Elsewhere, the settled Berber villagers had been obliged to adapt to the increasing power of the nomadic Berber tribes while farming declined as nomadism increased.

While North Africa's Christian inhabitants were largely concentrated in towns and ports, one of the most fascinating features of what are now Morocco and Algeria during this period was the rise of Jewish Berber tribes such as the Mediouno of the Oran area, the Riata of the Rif mountains, the Fazaz and Fandalu of north-western Morocco. How and when they converted to Judaism is unclear but they apparently achieved a degree of domination over some pagan Berber tribes. It has even been suggested that, around AD 694, these Moroccan Jews sent a force to help their persecuted co-religionists in Iberia.

One of the most enigmatic wall paintings in the 8th-century Umayyad reception hall at Qusayr Amra shows six non-Islamic rulers, one of whom is identified as Roderick the last Visigothic king of Spain. They were once thought to represent kingdoms conquered by the Muslims, but in reality they probably represent 'The Family of the Rulers of the Earth' welcoming a new member, namely the Umayyad Caliphate itself. (*in situ* Qusayr Amra, Jordan; author's photograph)

The Maghrib and al-Andalus, *c.* AD 731

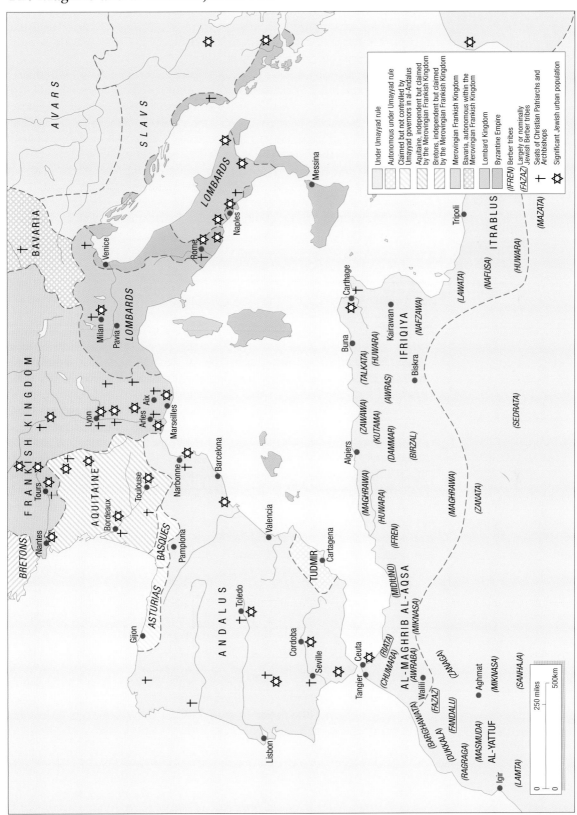

Legend:

- Under Umayyad rule
- Autonomous under Umayyad rule
- Claimed but not controlled by Umayyad governors in al-Andalus
- Aquitaine, independent but claimed by the Merovingian Frankish Kingdom
- Bretons, independent but claimed by the Merovingian Frankish Kingdom
- Merovingian Frankish Kingdom
- Bavaria, autonomous within the Merovingian Frankish Kingdom
- Lombard Kingdom
- Byzantine Empire
- (IFREN) Berber tribes
- (FAZAZ) Largely or nominally Jewish urban population
- ✝ Seats of Christian Patriarchs and Archbishops
- ✡ Significant Jewish urban population

AVARS

SLAVS

BAVARIA

LOMBARDS

Messina

Naples

Rome

Venice

Milan

Pavia

LOMBARDS

FRANKISH KINGDOM

Lyon

Aix

Arles

Marseilles

Barcelona

AQUITAINE

Toulouse

Bordeaux

Narbonne

BASQUES

Nantes

BRETONS

Pamplona

Valencia

Cartagena

TUDMIR

ASTURIAS

Gijon

ANDALUS

Toledo

Cordoba

Seville

Ceuta

Tangier

Lisbon

AL-MAGHRIB AL-AQSA

(MIDIUNO)

(RIATA)

(CHUMARA)

(AWRABA)

(MIKNASA)

(ZANAGA)

(FAZAZ)

Wallili

Aghmat

(FANDALU)

(MASMUDA)

(BARGHWANATA)

(DUKKALA)

(RAGRAGA)

AL-YATTUF

(LAMTA)

Igir

(SANHAJA)

Carthage

Kairawan

IFRIQIYA

Buna

Biskra

(NAFZAWA)

(HUWARA)

(TALKATA)

(AWRAS)

(DAMMAR)

(KUTAMA)

(ZAWAWA)

Algiers

(BIRZAL)

(MAGHRAWA)

(HUWARA)

(IFREN)

(ZANATA)

(MAGHRAWA)

(SEDRATA)

Tripoli

ITRABLUS

(MAZATA)

(HUWARA)

(NAFUSA)

(LAWATA)

0   250 miles
0   500km

11

The entire area from Libyan Tripoli to Morocco became the Umayyad province of Ifriqiya with its capital in Tunisia. However, there was very little Arab settlement of North Africa until the mid-11th century, and, in this region of al-Maghrib, 'The West', the Arabs remained a small but dominant elite. The first Berber tribes to convert to Islam were the pagan Masmuda of the plains, perhaps because of their opposition to the Christians of the towns and Jews of the hills. Thereafter Berber nomads became Muslim faster than the Christian villages did, while the towns converted last; the resulting period of accommodation between a Berber majority and a ruling Arab minority worked quite well until the AD 730s.

There were several reasons for an underlying tension between Arabs and Berbers, not least because the Arabs imposed more taxes than were allowed under Islamic *Sharia* law. Worse still, Berbers serving in Muslim armies often received inferior pay even after converting to Islam and becoming *mawali* 'clients' of a dominant Arab group (see below). Unequal treatment continued under the Caliph Hisham and eventually led to a massive Berber rebellion.

The Muslim conquest of al-Andalus had been carried out with an invasion force of around 15,000 troops, mostly Berbers under Arab command plus an elite of Arab troops from the provincial forces of North Africa. It has also been suggested that two of the first Muslim commanders to cross the Straits of Gibraltar, Tarif and Tariq, had already been there as part of previous Jewish Berber raids. The subsequent Muslim conquest of the Visigothic Kingdom was rapid and at first, perhaps, unofficial. It clearly came as something of a surprise to the Umayyad Government in Syria which, after suffering naval defeats by the Byzantines, even considered withdrawing Islamic forces because they were separated from the rest of the caliphate by sea.

There was no withdrawal; instead Arabs and Berbers replaced the Germanic Visigoths as a dominant military and ruling class. However, the Umayyad governorate, as distinct from the subsequent independent Andalusian Umayyad state, remains a confused period. Not only was there competition between the Qays and Kalb, but also between Arabs and Berbers. From the assassination of the first *wali* or governor in AD 716 until the death of Abd al-Rahman al-Ghafiqi at the battle of Poitiers in AD 732, only one governor remained in post for more than five years, most holding authority for six months or less. Nevertheless, most governors worked hard to consolidate Muslim control within the Iberian Peninsula while also raiding the lands north of the Pyrenees.

Despite political tumult within al-Andalus, several campaigns were launched into the north-east, into what later became Aragon and Catalonia as well as the fertile and urbanized Ebro Valley where Umayyad armies could easily be reinforced by sea from the Mediterranean. It is less clear what was happening in the north and north-west though archaeological evidence suggests that the local population remained in place while the old Christian aristocracy was largely replaced by Muslim Berbers who subsequently abandoned the area, themselves being replaced by a new Christian ruling class.

The region that the Romans had known as Septimania, along the Mediterranean coast of France north of the Pyrenees, was very different. Fertile, urbanized, with a Mediterranean climate and flourishing trade links with southern and western Europe as well as North Africa and the Middle East, it was a prize worth defending. So, after the Visigothic King Roderick had been killed at the battle of Guadalete in AD 711 a certain Achila succeeded him before eventually seeking refuge in Narbonne, in the still-

Visigothic province of Septimania. However, Muslim forces soon marched north of the Pyrenees and in AD 719 they took control of Narbonne. Nearby Carcassone, however, did not fall to the Muslims until AD 725 when its surrender marked the definitive end of the Visigothic state.

Meanwhile, much of the Visigothic military aristocracy remained in Septimania alongside the new Umayyad garrisons.

Until Abd al-Rahman al-Ghafiqi broke with tradition and launched an attack across the western Pyrenees, all previous raids had set out from Septimania. East of the independent Basque country, most of the mountains had been under at least nominal Visigothic rule, plus the coastal region of Septimania, and the Umayyad *walis* who now governed clearly wanted to incorporate all of what had been the Visigothic Kingdom.

Campaigns beyond such frontiers were commonplace, but formed part of a strategy of softening up enemy states which would not be followed by campaigns of conquests until the foe had been sufficiently weakened. Muslim attacks on Avignon and Lyon in the Rhône Valley fitted this pattern whereas the attack on Toulouse, launched by governor al-Samh in AD 721 may have been an attempt at conquest. Its failure and the death of al-Samh were thus seen as a more significant defeat that the subsequent Muslim failure at the battle of Poitiers. The army that tried to seize Toulouse was much larger, with numerous siege engines and appears to have been accompanied by the soldiers' families, which was why its defeat by Prince Eudes of Aquitaine resulted in such appalling levels of casualties. It was Abd al-Rahman al-Ghafiqi who took command after al-Samh's death and led the Muslim Army's remnants back to Septimania, whereupon the Muslims of al-Andalus selected him as their governor. However, this did not last long because the governor of Ifriqiya replaced al-Ghafiqi with one of his own men, Anbasa Ibn Suhaym al-Kalbi.

Eudes' victory greatly strengthened his position in Aquitaine where Visigothic refugees from the south and Frankish exiles from the north may already have boosted his military potential. That may have been why the next Muslim raids were directed north-eastwards towards the ill-defended Rhône Valley. Even so, four years passed before Governor Anbasa conducted an astonishingly far-ranging campaign that penetrated up the Rhône and Saône valleys as far as Autun.

There was nevertheless already disunity in the Muslim ranks. According to the anonymous *Mozarab Chronicle*, written by an Andalusian Christian scribe in AD 754, Munusa, the Berber governor of the Cerdagne region of the eastern Pyrenees reacted to the 'oppression' of his fellow Berbers by the Arabs and 'made peace with the Franks', this rebellion against Umayyad authority predated the great Berber uprisings in North Africa and al-Andalus by several years. Munusa may originally have been the governor of a frontier area farther west and been defeated by Pelagius at Covadonga in AD 718 or 722. According to al-Maqqari, the *wali* Haytham Ibn Ubayda defeated Munusa in AD 729 but this Berber rebel still controlled the Cerdagne frontier zone when Abd al-Rahman al-Ghafiqi again became governor.

MEROVINGIAN FRANCE AND AQUITAINE

The immediate background to the battle of Poitiers can be found in the recently conquered Umayyad province of al-Andalus and within France itself. What is clear is that the confrontation between Franks and Umayyads was not simply a clash between Christianity and Islam but resulted from political rivalry and was in many ways a clash between Germanic northern and Mediterranean southern Europe. Aquitaine was caught firmly in the middle of this clash, and it is certainly worth noting that Aquitainian sources often referred to Franks as *barbari*, 'barbarians'.

'Barbarian' or not, the Merovingian Frankish Kingdom had long been the dominant Christian power in Western Europe. Though currently in decline, it would soon be rebuilt by Charles Martel and his descendants in the form of a Carolingian Frankish Empire. The Germanic Franks who now dominated most of France, western Germany and the Low Countries had still not been entirely converted to Christianity by the early 8th century AD. Their state, while dominating several other Germanic 'barbarian' kingdoms, was itself divided into Austrasia in the east and Neustria in the west; Austrasia being the main power base of the Pepinid mayors of the palace, a dynasty of military dictators descended from Pepin of Heristal and currently represented by Charles Martel. Having won a civil war to secure his position as mayor of the palace in both Austrasia and Neustria, Charles Martel concentrated upon eastern and northern campaigns against largely pagan Frisians and Saxons as well as fellow-Christian Alamans and Bavarians. One of Charles Martel's few

The great early medieval churches of Aquitaine were fabulously wealthy, which was one reason why they became targets of 'Saracen' and other raids. The gold and inlaid reliquary of Sainte-Foy in the Abbey of Conques dates from some years after the battle of Poitiers but is a typical example of the portable booty the raiders were looking for. (Treasury, Abbey of Sainte-Foy, Conques)

The Merovingian Frankish Kingdom, *c.* AD 731

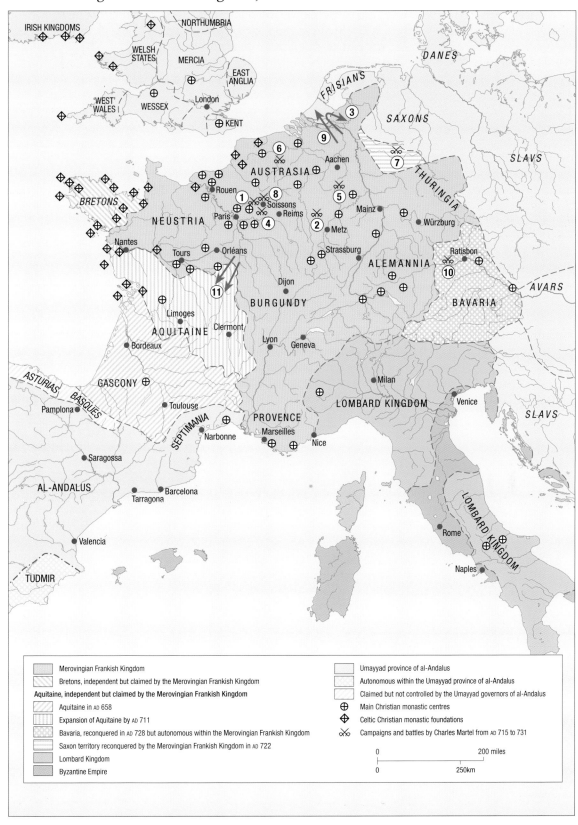

IRISH KINGDOMS

NORTHUMBRIA

WELSH STATES

MERCIA

EAST ANGLIA

DANES

'WEST' WALES

WESSEX

London

KENT

FRISIANS

SAXONS

SLAVS

AUSTRASIA

Aachen

THURINGIA

Rouen

Soissons

Reims

Mainz

Würzburg

NEUSTRIA

Paris

Metz

BRETONS

Strassburg

ALEMANNIA

Ratisbon

AVARS

Nantes

Tours

Orléans

Dijon

BURGUNDY

BAVARIA

Limoges

Clermont

Lyon

Geneva

AQUITAINE

Bordeaux

Milan

Venice

SLAVS

ASTURIAS

BASQUES

GASCONY

Pamplona

Toulouse

SEPTIMANIA

Narbonne

PROVENCE

Marseilles

Nice

LOMBARD KINGDOM

Saragossa

AL-ANDALUS

Tarragona

Barcelona

Rome

LOMBARD KINGDOM

Valencia

Naples

TUDMIR

	Merovingian Frankish Kingdom		Umayyad province of al-Andalus
	Bretons, independent but claimed by the Merovingian Frankish Kingdom		Autonomous within the Umayyad province of al-Andalus
Aquitaine, independent but claimed by the Merovingian Frankish Kingdom			Claimed but not controlled by the Umayyad governors of al-Andalus
	Aquitaine in AD 658	⊕	Main Christian monastic centres
	Expansion of Aquitaine by AD 711	⊕	Celtic Christian monastic foundations
	Bavaria, reconquered in AD 728 but autonomous within the Merovingian Frankish Kingdom	✂	Campaigns and battles by Charles Martel from AD 715 to 731
	Saxon territory reconquered by the Merovingian Frankish Kingdom in AD 722		
	Lombard Kingdom		
	Byzantine Empire		

0   200 miles

0   250km

western campaigns was a siege of Angers in AD 724, where Rainfroi, an ex-mayor of the Neustrian Palace, had rebelled against his authority.

Aquitaine remained one of the most Romanized regions of what is now France. Around AD 714 its ruler Eudes felt strong enough to proclaim himself an independent prince rather than a Frankish vassal. Its largely Gallo-Roman and emphatically Christian population enjoyed a degree of civilization superior to that of Frankish Neustria and more backward Austrasia. The Roman towns had survived and in some cases even expanded beyond their late Roman fortifications, with the 6th century AD having been a period of new building and the restoration of ancient churches. Aquitaine was also rich in mineral resources, including silver and gold.

Aquitaine initially seems to have become a significant regional power under a certain Duke Felix, 'a very noble and illustrious patrician from the town of Toulouse' whose protégé Lupus then became prince and, according to Frankish accounts, 'rebelled' against the Merovingian Frankish king towards the close of the 7th century AD. The early 8th century AD then saw Aquitaine expand north and east while the Merovingian Kingdom teetered on the brink of fragmentation. This was not, however, simply an anti-Frankish phenomenon, since Franks who had earlier settled in Aquitaine continued to serve their new non-Frankish ruler. There were also substantial Visigothic communities close to the until recently Visigothic – now Umayyad – province of Septimania and in the Pyrenean foothills. Such families of Germanic Goth or Frank origin probably formed local aristocracies or military elites.

The most significant military relationship was, however, that between the Gallo-Roman Aquitainians, the largely Christian Gascons and the largely pagan Basques of the south-west. In fact the Aquitainian reliance upon Basque soldiers often caused their northern foes to refer to all Aquitainians as *Vascones* whom these northern chroniclers also described as an 'an evil nation'. On the other hand a growing sense of separate identity had already led the people of this area to refer to themselves as *Aquitani*.

With the principality of Aquitaine now controlling south-western France it is hardly surprising that the Frankish mayor of the palace, Charles Martel, feared an alliance between Prince Eudes and the Burgundians, who were also attempting to throw off Frankish domination in south-eastern France. While Charles probably ensured that the strategic frontier city of Tours was properly defended because it controlled territory on both sides of the Loire River, several powerful bishops including those of Auxerre and Orléans on the Loire also commanded substantial local militias.

On the south-western frontier of Aquitaine lay the territory of the largely pagan Basque tribes who, in the late 7th century AD had emerged from the Pyrenees to overrun much of *Vasconia* or Gascony. Warlike and usually independent, the Basques remained troublesome neighbours for the Visigothic kings and for the Umayyad governors who replaced them. For the rulers of Aquitaine, however, they were a vitally important source of troops, though this did not stop some Basque chieftains making peace with the newly arrived Muslim conquerors. Some converted to Islam and paid tribute in return for retaining sovereignty within their mountains. One such was Fortunio of the Borja district of Navarre who, in AD 715, founded the Arabized 'dynasty' of the *Bani Lupo*, which surely had links with the Gascon dynasty of Lupus or Loup.

CHRONOLOGY

710 Roderick becomes king of the Visigoths but Visigothic nobles in Septimania rebel and proclaim the previous ruler's son Akhila; first Muslim raid against Iberia (July); Duke Lupus I of Gascony is deposed or dies and Eudes takes control of Gascony as well as Aquitaine.

711 Muslim invasion of Visigothic Iberia, Roderick defeated at battle of Guadalete; peaceful relations between Franks and Frisians consolidated by marriage between Pepin of Heristal's brother Grimoald to the daughter of a Frisian leader, Radbod Theudesinde.

712 Musa Ibn Nusayr, the Umayyad governor of North Africa, joins in the conquest of the Iberian Peninsula.

713 Final defeat of the Visigothic Kingdom at the battle of Segoyuela; Visigothic Prince Theodimir of Murcia makes peace with the Muslims and is permitted to retain his authority in the area subsequently known as Tudmir.

714 Continuing campaigns confirm Muslim domination of Iberia; perhaps legendary raid into France by Tarik Ibn Ziyad; Franks fortify the Rhône Valley; Musa Ibn Nusayr's son, Abd al-Aziz, is made *wali* of Andalus with his capital at Seville; in Septimania local Visigothic nobles of the anti-Roderick party are offered provisions similar to those of Theodimir of Murcia and accept Muslim overlordship; other Septimanian Visigoths revolt and proclaim a certain Ardo as king; other Visigothic refugees gather in the Picos de Europa mountains of Asturias; death of Pepin of Heristal, mayor of the Merovingian palace, his infant grandson Theobald becoming nominal mayor of the palace while his repudiated wife Plectrude holds actual power and imprisons Pepin's illegitimate son Charles (the future Martel); civil war within the Pepinid clan; revolt by Neustrian Franks and Frisians; Duke Eudes proclaims himself the independent prince of Aquitaine.

715 Death of Umayyad Caliph Walid, succeeded by Sulayman; Charles (Martel) is freed, proclaimed mayor of the palace and defeats the army of Plectrude and the Neustrians at the battle of Cuisse-la-Motte; another victory at Verdun earns Charles his nickname of Martel, the 'blacksmith's hammer'; Charles Martel unsuccessfully attacks the Frisians.

716 Governor Abd al-Aziz of al-Andalus is assassinated; Ayyub Ibn Habib al-Lakhmi is interim *wali* for six months until replaced by al-Hurr Ibn Abd al-Rahman al-Thaqafi who moves the capital to Cordoba; Charles Martel defeats Frisian raiders near Malmedy.

717 Death of Caliph Sulayman, Umar Ibn Abd al-Aziz becomes Umayyad caliph; first confirmed Muslim expedition into Septimania which was ruled by King Ardo; Charles Martel defeats alliance of Neustrians and Aquitainians at the battle of Crèvecoeur-sur-l'Escaut near Cambrai (21 March) followed by another victory near Soissons, confirming Austrasian domination within the Merovingian Frankish Kingdom; Charles Martel turns east to face problems with the Saxons; Rainfroi, the ex-mayor of the Neustrian palace flees to Angers.

718 Traditional date when Pelagius (Don Pelayo) is proclaimed *caudillo* by the assembly of Asturias, he establishes a base at Cangas de Onís, defeating an attempt by the local Muslim governor and the Christian metropolitan of Seville to arrest him; Charles Martel repulses Saxons on river Weser.

719 First major Muslim attack upon Visigothic Septimania, Governor al-Samh takes or re-takes Narbonne before raiding Toulouse area; King Ardo of Septimania overthrown by Muslims (or AD 720); Charles Martel meets Prince Eudes of Aquitaine and the nominal Merovingian King Chilperic II at another battle of Soissons (March) with inconclusive results; Frisian resistance fragments on the death of their leader Radbod.

720 Death of Caliph Umar Ibn Abd al-Aziz, Yazid II becomes Umayyad caliph. Possible start of prolonged Muslim siege of Carcassonne.

During the early medieval period, especially when southern France was subjected to repeated Muslim raids, many large Roman structures were converted into fortresses. One was the Triumphal Arch at Orange, at the southern end of the Rhône Valley, as shown in this 18th-century engraving. (Author's collection)

Unfortunately, the 19th-century passion for restoring all things 'classical' resulted in the early medieval fortifications on top of the Roman arch at Orange being demolished. (Author's photograph)

721 Muslim invasion defeated by Prince Eudes of Aquitaine outside Toulouse, death of al-Samh, the governor of al-Andalus (11 March or 9/10 June); Anbasa Ibn Suhaym al-Kalbi become governor of al-Andalus; Thierry IV becomes king of the Franks (or perhaps in AD 720); start of a sequence of campaigns by Charles Martel to restore the authority of the palace throughout the Frankish Kingdom, including against Frankish-claimed Aquitaine and Provence; Charles exiles Bishop Rigobert of Rheims, a supporter of Rainfroi who seeks refuge with Prince Eudes.

722 Pelagius defeats Muslim force at Alqama, traditionally marking start of the 'Reconquista' (28 May).

724 Rainfroi 'rebels' against Charles Martel; Charles Martel defeats Frisians and Saxons; death of Caliph Yazid II, Hisham I becomes Umayyad caliph; Muslim fleets raid Sardinia, Corsica and the Balearic Islands.

725 Last Visigothic garrisons expelled from Carcassonne and Nîmes; raid by governor Anbasa up the Rhône and Saône valleys into Burgundy, taking Autun (22 August), traditionally reaching Luxeuil and Sens while some raiders may have reached the Vosges Mountains; Charles Martel meanwhile defeats Bavarians; Prince Eudes seeks an alliance with the Muslim governor of Cerdagne, currently in rebellion against the central government in Cordoba (probably not cemented until AD 729)

726 Death of *wali* Anbasa Ibn Suhaym al-Kalbi, briefly succeeded by Udhra Ibn Abd Allah al-Fihri before Yahya Ibn Salama al-Kalbi becomes governor of al-Andalus; further Muslim raids, perhaps by Abd al-Rahman al-Ghafiqi as governor of Narbonne.

728 Yahya Ibn Salama al-Kalbi replaced as governor of al-Andalus by Hudhaifa Ibn al-Alhwas al-Kaisi who was himself replaced later same year by Uthman Ibn Abi Nis'a al-Khath'ami.

729   Uthman Ibn Abi Nis'a al-Khath'ami replaced as governor of Andalus by al-Haitham Ibn Ubaid al-Kilabi.

729   Alliance between Prince Eudes of Aquitaine and Munusa, the rebel Berber governor of Cerdagne, said to be cemented by marriage between Munusa and Eudes' illegitimate daughter.

730   Al-Haitham replaced as governor of al-Andalus by Muhammad Ibn Abd Allah al-Ashja'a who is himself replaced later in the year by Abd al-Rahman al-Ghafiqi; successful Muslim naval raid against Byzantine-ruled Sicily.

731   Reinforcements arrive in al-Andalus from North Africa for a major campaign the following year; al-Ghafiqi crushes rebellion by Munusa in the Cerdagne; Muslim garrisons in Septimania may have raided Arles around the time of the defeat of Munusa; Muslim raiders defeat local force headed by local bishop named Emiland at Saint-Emiland near Couches (22 August); meeting between Eudes and Rainfroi makes Charles Martel fear an alliance against him; Charles exiles Rainfroi's supporter, Abbot Wandon of Fontenelle, and imprisons Bishop Aimar of Auxerre; two raids by Charles Martel across Loire into Berry region of Aquitaine.

732   Muslim Army under Abd al-Rahman al-Ghafiqi crosses western Pyrenees, raids across much of Gascony and Aquitaine (May–June); other units possibly enter Aquitaine via the eastern Pyrenean passes, Septimania and by sea from Tarragona; Gascon forces are mobilized by Eudes and muster close to the Garonne; Prince Eudes' Army defeated outside Bordeaux, Bordeaux falls and is sacked (June); Eudes regroups near the Dordogne but is again defeated and withdraws across the Loire, seeking support from Charles Martel; Muslims ravage Périgueux, Saintes and Angoulême then sack the Basilica of Saint-Hilaire outside Poitiers; Muslims continue north towards the Basilica of Saint-Martin outside Tours.

Charles Martel raises a massive army, crosses the Loire at Orléans and makes camp outside Tours; after initial clashes al-Ghafiqi pulls back to establish a position between the Clain and Vienne rivers; followed by Charles Martel; several days' stand-off followed by the battle of Poitiers (25 October); the Franks are driven off but Abd al-Rahman al-Ghafiqi is killed and the Muslim Army withdraws southwards to Septimania; a separate part of the Muslim Army probably pulls back along the road it originally came across the Pyrenean mountains; Prince Eudes pursues the main Muslim force via La Marche before returning to Bordeaux;

Charles Martel withdraws to Frankish territory through Orléans and Auxerre, demoting those bishops whom he thought unreliable; Abd al-Malik Ibn Katan al-Fihri becomes the new *wali* of al-Andalus; a separate Muslim force raids the Rhône region, perhaps in alliance with the Duke of Burgundy who wanted to assert his independence from the Franks; major Muslim naval raids against Sicily and Sardinia.

Spring, end of major Khazar offensive against Muslims on the central front.

733   Probable date of abdication of Eudes of Aquitaine, his lands being divided between his sons Hunald and Hatton who continue the conflict with Charles Martel; battles at Benest in Charente and La Rochefoucauld near Angoulême where Charles Martel probably defeats the Aquitainians; Charles Martel also campaigns against the Burgundians.

734   Yusuf Ibn Abd al-Rahman, the governor of Septimania, raids the Rhône Valley, Arles is handed over by Count Mauront who is in rebellion against Charles Martel; raiders also attack up the Durance valley; Abd al-Malik Ibn Qatan al-Fihri replaced as *wali* of Andalus by Uqba Ibn al-Hajjaj al-Saluli with orders to control the troublesome Berbers but this stimulates a Berber revolt; Ubaydullah Ibn al-Habhab al-Mawsili is made governor of North Africa with the same orders; Charles Martel sends a combined land and seaborne campaign against the Frisians.

736   Muslims defeated by Charles Martel at Sernhac near Beaucaire (6 August); Charles Martel imposes Frankish domination on Provence.

737   Muslims take Avignon and Provençals throw off Frankish domination; Charles Martel retakes Avignon from Muslims, unsuccessfully besieges Narbonne but defeats a relief army near the river Berre; death of King Pelagius of Asturias who is succeeded by his son Favila.

738   Charles Martel campaigns against the Saxons.

739   After a peace accord with the Lombards in Italy, Charles Martel attacks Duke Mauronte of Provence and his Muslim allies; death of King Favila of Asturias, succeeded by Alfonso I.

740   Kulthum Ibn Iyad al-Qasri (or al-Qashayri) is made *wali* of North Africa; widespread Berber revolt; al-Saluli, the *wali* of al-Andalus is defeated at the battle of the Nobles near Tangier (winter AD 740/41), seriously undermining Arab domination in Islamic North Africa; Berber revolt in North Africa sparks Berber revolt in al-Andalus, causing the Umayyad governor to withdraw troops from many garrisons north of the Pyrenees (these Berber revolts not defeated until AD 742).

OPPOSING COMMANDERS

CHRISTIAN

According to the medieval *Chronicle of Saint-Denis* **Charles Martel** got his nickname because: 'as a *martel* [hammer] breaks and crushes iron, steel and all other metals, so did he break up and crush his enemies'. Born around AD 688, Charles was the father of the Carolingian dynasty that ruled France until the late 10th century though, until Pepin the Short dethroned the last Merovingian king in AD 752, they ruled as mayors of the palace rather than kings.

Charles was himself the illegitimate son of Pepin II of Heristal, the mayor of the Merovingian palaces of Austrasia, Neustria and Burgundy. When Pepin II died in AD 714, leaving only grandchildren as legitimate heirs, a power struggle within the Frankish Kingdom was accompanied by Frisian and Aquitainian invasions. Helped by his Austrasian relatives, Charles defeated his rivals and by AD 723 established himself as sole mayor of the palace under the nominal rule of King Thierry IV.

He fought successive, and usually successful, wars against the neighbouring Frisians, Saxons and Alemanni, as well as supporting Anglo-Saxon missionaries as part of his effort to both Christianize and dominate the pagan German tribes east of the Frankish Kingdom. Charles Martel died in AD 741, nine years after his famous victory over Muslim raiders at the battle of Poitiers, and was buried in the Merovingian royal chapel at Saint-Denis outside Paris, a privilege reflecting his status as the greatest of all the mayors of the Merovingian palaces.

Eudes first appeared in the records as 'Eudo, prince of the province of Aquitaine' around the year AD 700. However, this was written years later and AD 700 seems too early for Eudes to have been in a real position of power. Local sources portrayed him as a 'Roman' fighting the *barbari*, by which Aquitainian chroniclers meant the Franks. Though nothing is known for certain about his origins, his supporters made much of Eudes' Gallo-Roman culture and the Gallo-Roman character of his army.

One story linked his father with the Lupus clan, which had featured in Gascon, Basque and northern Spanish history before, during and after the Islamic conquest of the Iberian Peninsula. In AD 710 or 719 a Gascon ruler known as Lupus I, having taken over from an even more obscure duke named Felix, either died or was deposed, having already lost Aquitaine to Eudes who now took over as duke of both Gascony and Aquitaine. What is clear is that Eudes expanded Aquitaine and, following the death of Pepin the mayor of the

The front and back of a coin minted during the period when Charles Martel was mayor of the Merovingian Frankish palace; in effect ruler of the kingdom whereas the king was little more than a figurehead. (Author's collection)

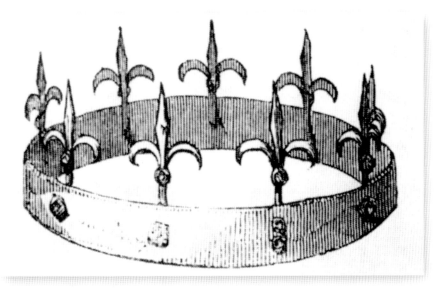

An early 19-century engraving of the now-lost crown of Prince Eudes or of his son Hunald when they ruled the independent principality of Aquitaine. The pointed fleurs-de-lis were almost certainly added at a later date, but the simple gold circlet might well have dated from the 8th century AD. (Author's collection)

Merovingian palace, Eudes was proclaimed *princeps* of Aquitaine, thereby asserting legal as well as practical independence from the Frankish Kingdom. Within a few years he was also vigorously involved in the civil wars that threatened to tear the Merovingian Frankish Kingdom apart.

In AD 721 Prince Eudes also defeated an invading Muslim army outside Toulouse, thus greatly boosting his own prestige, and by the end of that decade Eudes ruled virtually all the provinces south and west of the river Loire, except for the region around the strategic city of Tours. In fact, until his defeat by Abd al-Rahman al-Ghafiqi in AD 732, Prince Eudes rivalled Charles Martel as the strongest effective ruler in France. He died in AD 735 and was remembered in Aquitaine as the hero of the struggle against the 'Saracens', his achievements contributing to a growing sense of separate Aquitainian identity.

Thierry IV was the nominal Merovingian king of Neustria and Burgundy at the time of the battle of Poitiers, ruling from AD 720 until 737. But his power was nonexistent and his prestige even lower than that of most of the rest of the enfeebled late Merovingian kings whom French history dismisses as *Les Rois Fainéants*, the 'idle kings'. His immediate predecessors had similarly been tools in the hands of competing mayors of the Merovingian palaces, especially during the conflicts between Austrasia and Neustria.

During the civil war which followed the death of the great Mayor Pepin of Heristal, the Neustrian Franks took advantage of the death of the nominal King Dabodert III in AD 715, to bring one of the earlier King Childeric II's sons out of his monastic retreat and proclaim him as Chilperic III. Meanwhile Pepin of Heristal's illegitimate but energetic son Charles (Martel) defeated the Neustrians and proclaimed another member of the Merovingian royal family as the rival King Clotaire IV. He proved so incapable that Charles restored him to his monastery. In AD 721 Charles looked for another malleable Merovingian and found a supposed son of Thierry III in the monastery of Chelles, who thus became King Thierry IV who 'ruled' until his death in AD 737. In fact this Thierry was so insignificant that Charles Martel did not even bother to replace him, but neither did he seize the crown, resulting in a six-year interregnum when the Merovingian Kingdom got along quite well without a Merovingian king, ending with the coronation of the last Merovingian king, Childeric III, known as 'the Idiot'.

MUSLIM

Abd al-Rahman Ibn Abd Allah al-Ghafiqi, (referred to as Abd al-Rahman al-Ghafiqi) commander of the army that invaded France in AD 732 was, as his name indicated, from the Ghafiq clan, one of the Arab clans or sub-tribes that settled in al-Andalus at an early date. They were part of the Kalb tribal federation and reportedly formed one-third of the Arab warriors who had conquered Egypt in the mid-7th century AD. A relatively small number came to the Iberian Peninsula as part of Musa Ibn Nusayr's invading army.

One of these *baladiyun*, first conquerors and settlers, was probably Abd al-Rahman Ibn Abd Allah himself. He first appeared in the written sources during the disastrous siege of Toulouse in AD 721 and was credited with returning the defeated army to Narbonne. Under the Umayyad command structure, a military commander would designate one or more successors in case he himself was killed, and this was probably how al-Ghafiqi briefly became *wali* of al-Andalus. However, he was not acceptable to the governor of North Africa who also had overall responsibility for al-Andalus, supposedly because al-Ghafiqi was too generous to the defeated troops, so Anbasa Ibn Suhaym al-Kalbi replaced him. In reality this change probably reflected rivalry between the Qays and Kalb tribal factions.

The smashed and partially restored stucco statuette of a man with a sword which originally stood above the entrance to the palace complex built for the Caliph Hisham at Khirbat al-Mafjir in Palestine. It probably represented the Umayyad caliph but may not have been a portrait of Hisham himself. (Rockefeller Museum, Jerusalem)

Abd al-Rahman al-Ghafiqi was also noted for piety and was considered one of the *tabi'un*, 'disciples', who formed a kind of religious aristocracy within Islam, second only to the *ansar*, 'helpers', or *sabaha*, 'companions', who had known the Prophet Muhammad personally. According to the historian al-Maqqari, al-Ghafiqi's prestige also stemmed from the fact that he was a close friend of one of the sons of Umar, the second *Rashidun* or 'rightly guided' caliph.

Between his two terms as governor of al-Andalus, al-Ghafiqi served as a subordinate *wali* in Narbonne and 'the area at the foot of the Pyrenees'. During the crisis that followed Caliph Hisham's dismissal of the oppressive governor Haitham ibn Ubaid, the caliph's emissary to al-Andalus consulted the troops who overwhelmingly favoured the pious, honest, generous and brave al-Ghafiqi, who was also supported by the religious establishment. Nevertheless, as governor of al-Andalus he had two masters – the senior governor of North Africa and the caliph himself in distant Damascus. Though killed at the battle of Poitiers in AD 732, al-Ghafiqi's reputation remained intact and was even inherited by his descendants who continued to live at Murniyanat al-Ghafiqiyun west of Seville.

Abu'l-Walid Hisham Ibn Abd al-Malik was the tenth caliph of the Umayyad dynasty. Usually known simply as Hisham, he was born in Damascus in AD 691, the son of Caliph Abd al-Malik and a noble Arab lady named A'isha Bint Hisham. His elder brothers al-Walid and Sulayman were caliphs before him but were succeeded by

Umar Ibn Abd al-Aziz, then Hisham's third brother, Yazid II, until Hisham himself finally came to the throne in AD 724.

Caliph Hisham's long reign saw the end of the Umayyad dynasty's period of splendour, being followed by a steep decline and then the collapse of the dynasty itself in AD 750. It was also a time of dramatic events across the vast Umayyad state that stretched from India and Central Asia to the Atlantic. Nevertheless, Hisham tried to maintain Umayyad authority and was particularly concerned to maintain a balance between the rival Qays and Kalb tribal groups, while also supporting reforms to keep the Muslim but non-Arab *mawalis* content.

Hisham himself was described as a sober, frugal man and a strict administrator, his only ostentation being the Umayyad family's characteristic love of building. This resulted in numerous castles, palaces and new towns, some of which are only now being uncovered by archaeologists. In religion, Hisham was an orthodox Muslim, kindly towards Christians and Jews, with a deep interest in the history and traditions of pre-Islamic Iran.

The original Berber name of **Munusa**, Munuza or Manussa may have been Manresa and some sources described him as a great persecutor of the Christians during the early years of his career.

The figure of a man with a straight sword and scabbard at his side also appears on the early 8th-century Umayyad wall paintings at Qusayr Amra in Jordan, though this image had by now disappeared from Umayyad coinage. In each case the figure clearly shows a 'person of authority' who was not necessarily the caliph or a member of the Umayyad ruling family but represented the Ummayad Caliphate as a whole. (*in situ* Qusayr Amra, Jordan; author's photograph)

Al-Maqqari claimed that he had a bishop named Anambadus burned alive, though there is no record of such a bishop in the Christian sources. Other more legendary sources maintain that Munusa once commanded a huge swathe of the northern frontier of Umayyad al-Andalus and that Abd al-Rahman al-Ghafiqi ruined Munusa's dreams of power. Tensions between Arabs and Berbers may be the reality behind such stories, and it is possible that the Berber troops were further alienated when al-Ghafiqi became *wali* for the second time. But unfortunately the Arab sources rarely bothered to mention Berber attitudes until the latter exploded into a full-scale revolt

In reality, Munusa may have been a subordinate frontier governor north of Legio Septima (later known as León). According to the *Chronicle of Alfonso III*, written over a century later, a Muslim named Munusa fled from León after being defeated by Pelagius at Covodonga and was probably the same Munusa whom other Christian sources describe as governor of Cerritanensem, the Cerdagne or Puygcerda, who ruled from a strong location, the only weakness being its shortage of drinking water.

The story of Munusa's marriage to the beautiful but illegitimate daughter of Prince Eudes of Aquitaine has often been dismissed as legendary, though there is no reason why Eudes should not have strengthened his alliance with a formidable frontier chieftain by offering him a good-looking but low-status bride. The location of the rebels' mountain fastness, controlling at least one of the main passes between the Ebro plain and Septimania, would also have weighed upon al-Ghafiqi's mind.

OPPOSING FORCES

CHRISTIAN

It could be misleading to assume too much similarity between the armies of Charles Martel and his grandson, the Emperor Charlemagne, while a widespread belief that the 8th century AD saw the 'rise of cavalry' in Western Europe is also grossly oversimplified.

Charles Martel's military power initially consisted of little more than the Austrasian or eastern Frankish forces but, as he extended his authority, Charles installed new *leudes*, or governors, strengthened the military potential of frontier regions and used the administrative structures of the church as a framework for his military reforms. During this period the whole of society was affected by the demands of warfare, though this fell most heavily upon the military aristocracy. Charles Martel's conquests also offered opportunities for individual advancement and booty. Success bred success, attracting greater support so that within a quarter of a century Charles' initially small army became a significant weapon of conquest.

The strongly fortified town of Carcassone was one of the last parts of the province of Septimania to fall to the Muslims in AD 725, marking the final end of the Visigothic Kingdom. Its late Roman walls and towers, having been maintained in good repair throughout the early medieval period, are now surrounded by lower but thicker, later medieval fortifications. (Author's photograph)

An array of Frankish military equipment plus a work-axe dating from the Merovingian period. Most come from the eastern and northern parts of France where Germanic influence upon the design of Merovingian weaponry remained much stronger than in the west and south. (Musée de l'Armée, Paris; author's photograph)

Warriors were expected to equip themselves according to their wealth or status but in Charles Martel's time many still had to rely upon pillaging enemy territory for food. Nevertheless Charles Martel and his successors normally achieved a significant numerical superiority over their foes. All free men were trained in warfare to some extent, even if only through hunting wild animals for food and to defend their herds. While military service remained a legal duty, with a maximum of three months per year, many men were already making money payments instead, these provided Charles Martel with the cash to pay and equip the numerous willing volunteers. What resulted were highly motivated, almost professional armies, while the raising of a general levy of ill-trained, ill-equipped and sometimes unwilling conscripts remained rare.

Aristocratic landholders were not only expected to serve in person but also brought additional troops with them. Abbeys, as significant landholders, similarly provided a specific number of troops and, although clerics were exempted from military service, senior churchmen often commanded their own contingents. Meanwhile Austrasia, and particularly the region between the rivers Rhine and Meuse, remained Charles Martel's main source of military manpower, Germanic Frankish military traditions also having survived more strongly in Austrasia than in other parts of the Merovingian Kingdom. During the early centuries of Merovingian rule in what is now France, the Franks had absorbed many existing military forces, ranging from

late Roman cavalry regiments, local *laeti* levies, as well as Germanic, Alan, Sarmatian and other *foederati*. Even in places where Frankish or other German settlement had been strongest, it seems likely that local elites were 'Germanized' at least as often as they were replaced. As a result, much of Charles Martel's military aristocracy were of Gallo-Roman or mixed Frankish-Gallo-Roman origin. At the same time the military role of the senior clergy increased as bishops took on the responsibilities of local government and local defence. On the other hand the command structure of Charles Martel's armies still reflected a Germanic social stratification with descent from high status German ancestors carrying significant prestige even in the deep south where Frankish and Gothic settlement had been thinly spread.

Amongst the lesser-known and more fragmentary wall paintings found in the ruins of the fortified palace and garrison base of Qasr al-Hayr al-Gharbi in Syria is this representation of a man thoughtfully stroking his beard. The palace was built for the Umayyad Caliph Hisham around AD 727. (Syrian National Museum, Damascus; author's photograph)

The more prosperous a landholder, the more likely he would serve on horseback, though during the 8th century AD this did not mean that he was necessarily a cavalryman, the distinction between horse-owning mounted infantry and proper cavalry being blurred. This having been said, there was clear evidence for large numbers of mounted troops in several regions that had once been parts of the Roman Empire, including Neustria and Brittany in northern France. There was also a tradition of mounted warfare amongst both the Basques and the Visigoths.

The army of Aquitaine was not the same as that of the late Merovingian Frankish Kingdom, though there were similarities, for example in the vital role of local magnates and their armed retainers. Prince Eudes, like other rulers, had to win their support by offering gifts, land or status. Since the later 6th century AD many *civitates* – regions based upon Roman urban centres – had their own local military levies, especially in frontier regions. They maintained local order and took part in military operations, being expected to campaign 500km or so from home and remain in the field for up to three months. Those involved fed and equipped themselves, mostly being drawn from prosperous sections of society whose lands were worked by serfs or slaves. In emergencies a more general host was summoned from the poorer but still free *inferiores* or *pauperes*.

Although a local aristocracy had evolved during the 6th and 7th centuries AD through a combination of the old Gallo-Roman and the new Germanic elites, the Aquitainian Army was based upon late Roman or early Byzantine rather than Germanic principles. This even extended to the recruitment of 'barbarian' 'non-Romans' as *foederati*. Aquitaine had, in fact, suffered less devastating Germanic invasions following the collapse of the Western Roman Empire and still had relatively little contact with the ruling Frankish elites of the north.

Tensions with the Merovingian Kingdom did not stop Prince Eudes from employing Frankish troops. The most recent settlement by a Frankish nobility had been in the late 7th century AD, and these recent arrivals often seem to have been employed as urban garrisons. The *hostis Vascanorum* was similarly employed, though the confusion and overlap between the names Vasconian, Gascon and Basque makes it unclear whether such troops came from what is now Gascony or from the still largely pagan, semi-nomadic and tribal Basques of the mountains. The most important Aquitainian military units were the ruler's own *comitatus* or personal military following, and the garrisons based in or attached to the main cities.

The question of cavalry is again unclear, with the numerous references to mounted troops often perhaps referring to mounted infantry. Where the Basques were concerned, it can be stated with relative certainty that their mounted warriors habitually fought on horseback and this may also have been true of the Gascons, with both groups forming a vital element in Eudes' army.

Aquitaine bordered several potentially dangerous powers – notably the Franks and the Muslims. Partly as a result Aquitaine was divided into three duchies: Gascony in the south, the Toulousain in the south-west and the Auvergne in the east. There was also a frontier zone facing the independent Basques in the deep south while the fifth region facing the Franks along the Loire may not have been classed as a duchy. A *march* or frontier province facing the Bretons in the far north-west had recently fallen to the Franks. Upon these foundations, Prince Eudes and his successors built a defensive strategy largely relying upon urban fortifications and garrisons that worked well for several decades.

MUSLIM

At the time of the battle of Poitiers, the armies of the westernmost provinces of the Umayyad Caliphate consisted of two main groups; the indigenous Berbers of North Africa and the still largely Arab professional armies descended from, or consisting of, men of Middle Eastern origin.

The Alto de Perdon between Pamplona and Puente la Reina. The area between the river Ebro and Pamplona in northern Spain was a fertile region with good communications and close to passes through the Pyrenean Mountains, which was why Abd al-Rahman al-Ghafiqi assembled his army here before invading Aquitaine in AD 732. (Author's photograph)

Umayyad professional forces had changed considerably since the dynasty took over the caliphate following the initial wave of Arab-Islamic expansion in the mid-7th century AD. Although a significant role was still played by infantry archers and javelin throwers, most troops were now mounted infantry. Arab cavalry were still armed with spears and swords, rather than being horse-archers, but had learned much from their Iranian, Turkish and to a lesser extent Byzantine opponents. The Berbers and Germanic Visigoths of the west had virtually nothing to teach them.

The sprawling Umayyad Empire was no longer managed by manipulating kinship ties, as had been done in earlier decades, but instead major provincial governorships tended to be given to successful generals rather than kinsmen of the ruling caliph. Subordinate governorships went to military commanders on whom these generals could rely rather than tribal chiefs or kinsmen; this process was particularly obvious in North Africa and al-Andalus.

Meanwhile Arab tribal affiliation remained important because of competition for limited booty. As a result, competition between the largely mythical but still potent confederations of Qays and Kalb almost became a form of occasionally bloody power politics. This was reflected as much in the main regional armies of al-Andalus and North Africa, as it was elsewhere. Recruitment to these professional units had, however, changed since the early days of Islamic expansion. Enlistment was entirely voluntary and drew in both Arabs and non-Arabs, while the old tribal militias had already proved unwieldy and were increasingly marginalized, though not yet defunct.

Despite their astonishingly successful campaigns across a large part of the known world, early Muslim armies were remarkably small. By the 8th century AD available numbers had grown and later Umayyad military

The traditional Arab bows used by the earliest Islamic armies, and which continued to play a role amongst the infantry forces of the Umayyad Caliphate, were large weapons comparable to the later medieval, English, so-called longbow. One such weapon is carried by the Arab bedouin 'donor' on this 6th- or 7th-century mosaic. (*in situ* Kayanos Monastery Church, Mount Nebo, Jordan; Fr. Picirillo photograph)

potential may have been equivalent to that of the late Roman army, though such large numbers were rarely seen in North Africa and never in al-Andalus.

The basic Arabian tribal unit, or *ashira*, had proved too small to provide an effective operational formation so, under Umayyad rule, the tribes were reshaped into four or five large tribal divisions while new and almost artificial tribes or *qabilas* were created. This Umayyad break with a real tribal past was similarly seen in the replacement of smaller tribal armies by regular *ajnad* (sing. *jund*) regiments. Every *jund* had its *qa'id* commander who, by the later Umayyad period, was probably responsible for registering his *ashhab* (sing. *shihab*) troops with the government. Of these regional *jund* forces, only those in warlike or recently conquered frontier territory remained truly effective. There were also clear distinctions between distant provincial *jund* armies and the elite formations based in, or sent from, Syria.

Papyrus documents found in Egypt and dating from the Umayyad period suggest that troops were divided into small subsections, platoons and squads down to the ten-man *irafa*. Whether this was just for administrative purposes or was a tactical system for use on campaign is unknown. What is clear is that the Umayyad armies had a highly developed system of different sized flags and banners; the *liwa* signifying command while the *raya* was an emblem of a kinship group, regiment or senior individual.

The importance of infantry archery had declined by the mid-8th century AD, along with that of the less prestigious javelin, as the proportion of cavalry increased. Cavalry had played a minor role in the first Arab-Islamic conquests though had been more prominent in that of Egypt. Thereafter camel-riding infantry seem to have born the brunt of the conquest of North Africa whereas the conquest of al-Andalus and the subsequent raids into France differed because of the presence of large numbers of horse-riding Berber warriors.

In a professional, regular army such as that of the Umayyad Caliphate, money played an important role not only in covering the expenditures of warfare but also for maintaining morale through regular pay. Religion, however, remained the primary motivating factor. Of course there was also the possibility that loot and the desire for high-value booty could have a negative impact, as it seemingly did on the Poitiers campaign of AD 732. Writing a century later, the chronicler Ibn Abd al-Hakam, described how, during an Andalusian raid on Sardinia: 'a man drew his sword, took off the blade and threw it away, and placed the gold in the sheath, over which he replaced the hilt', thus effectively disarming himself in a way that his superiors could not see!

With such a sophisticated military machine at their disposal it is hardly surprising that Umayyad strategy was sometimes very sophisticated, not to say ambitious. In tactical terms, however, Umayyad traditions were less complex. In battle the early Muslim armies had often placed slingers as well as archers and perhaps javelin men on their flanks. Armoured men were placed in the front ranks, at least until armour became more abundant during the Umayyad Caliphate. During Hisham's reign substantial supplies of military equipment were sent from the main garrison centres to support provincial forces in time of need. It is, in fact, clear that later Umayyad armies no longer had much in common with the poorly equipped fighters of the first Islamic conquests. Each recruit was now issued with arms and armour, a horse on which to ride if not necessarily to fight, and a substantial sum in cash; all of which were required if he was to fulfil his role as a *muqatila* or professional soldier.

For many years the so-called 'Lombard Treasure' has been dismissed as late 19th- or early 20th-century fakes, not least because it contains sophisticated forms of one-piece iron helmets, which were thought not to exist during the early medieval period. More recent study has, however, shown that just this style of helmet was made and used by 8th-century Umayyad, perhaps Byzantine and probably Lombard armies. (Private collection)

Very few pictorial representations of armed men survive from North Africa around the time of the Arab-Islamic conquests, and even these tend to show the ruling Christian or ex-Byzantine elite rather than Berber tribal forces. One such survival is a 7th-century illustrated copy of the first five books of the Old Testament. The three figures shown here represent Pharaoh, Joseph and one of Pharaoh's men persecuting the Israelites. (*Ashburnham Pentateuch*, Bibliothèque Nationale, Nouv. Acq. Lat. 2334, 4. 58a, Paris, France)

The role of the fleet in support of Umayyad campaigns since the late 7th century AD clearly shows their appreciation of naval power. In fact, several Arab tribes of the Kalb faction had experience of seafaring in pre-Islamic times and some were settled along the Mediterranean coast of Egypt, primarily to defend Alexandria against Byzantine attack. Most of those involved served as marines while Christian Egyptian Copts served as sailors. Egypt had, in fact, been a major naval centre since early Umayyad times, and Egyptian papyri indicate that there were three fleets based on the river Nile, plus smaller squadrons to guard the delta. Part of this Egyptian Fleet may have raided the Iberian Peninsula as early as AD 647 during the initial Arab-Islamic invasion of North Africa.

Sabta (Ceuta) on the northern tip of Morocco may have been a Byzantine naval base during the 7th century AD. Located where the Mediterranean met the Atlanttic Ocean, Sabta and nearby Tangier also linked North Africa with the Iberian Peninsula. But quite why the first Muslim raiders needed ships from Count Julian of Tangier in order to reach Visigothic Spain in AD 710 is unclear, since there was already an Umayyad fleet operating in the western Mediterranean.

The Berbers of North Africa had only recently been drawn into the Islamic fold but were already a valuable source of military manpower at the time of the Poitiers campaign. Some had been loosely attached to an Arab tribe, or were inserted into pseudo-tribal regiments, as *mawalis* or 'clients' and as such played a major role in the Umayyad-Islamic conquest of the Iberian Peninsula. Musa Ibn Nusayr was himself of 'enslaved' or captive origin and most of Musa's *mawalis* were Berbers, plus some *Rumi* (Greeks or Byzantines) probably captured during the conquest of North Africa. There were also some Persians and others who may have remained slaves rather than being freed as *mawalis*. This *mawali* phenomenon was one of the most interesting aspects of early Islamic military history, perhaps resulting from the withering of real Arab tribes and tribal loyalties. Some entered the military system either as a full-blown *mawali* division consisting of regiments headed by a *qa'id*. This admission into the army changed a taxpayer into a tax-receiver as a salaried soldier, while even those not fully enrolled could become *mutatawwi'a*, unpaid irregular troops. Large numbers of such irregulars were certainly seen in the far western provinces of North Africa and al-Andalus.

The military heritage of the Berber tribal peoples of North Africa was quite complex, there having been many Syrian cavalry, archers and *dromedarii* – camel-mounted – infantry in this region during the period of the Roman Empire. In fact the adoption of the single-humped camel or dromedary then had a huge impact, enabling Berber nomads to penetrate and in many cases dominate previously settled agricultural territory. Thereafter the Berbers supplied *foederates* or local troops to the restored Romano-Byzantine Empire in the 6th and early 7th centuries AD.

Most of the Berber clans that are known to have taken part in the Islamic conquest of the Iberian Peninsula were from northern Morocco, particularly from the Zanata and Sanhaja tribal confederations. From an early date Umayyad governors encouraged the recruitment of Berbers and their conversion to Islam, but the number of such Berber families that settled in al-Andalus is much more debatable. In fact the evidence of place names within what are now Spain and Portugal suggests that their presence was temporary.

Various social, cultural and military differences distinguished the Berber tribes of the North African coasts from those in the mountains, steppes or desert fringes and desert proper. For example, most of the steppe tribes were sheep and goat herders while those of the mountains were more settled. All appeared very poor to outside observers though their leaderships had absorbed some degrees of Romano-Byzantine influence.

'The Holy Sepulchre', on a Carolingian ivory panel, 8th century AD. The sleeping guards' complete lack of armour was probably typical of the great majority of Charles Martel's army. (Bargello Mus., Florence; author's photograph)

Such Berber tribal forces included substantial numbers of unarmoured light cavalry and were almost certainly capable of fielding a larger proportion of cavalry than the Arabs. The motivation of Berber warriors under Islamic command was necessarily mixed. Those of *mawali* status generally proved loyal to their patron but little is known about their pay. The Umayyad caliphs tried to equalize the status and pay of Arabs and *mawalis* during the first half of the 8th century AD, this may have been more characteristic of the eastern provinces where most *mawalis* were the militarily more advanced Persians and Turks.

In tactical terms, Berber warfare was based upon *razzia* – raiding – similar to that of the early Arabs, though large Berber armies tended to go to war with their families, tents and flocks, and as a result were slow-moving. Their unarmoured cavalry primarily relied upon javelins and their tactics were a

Another page in the unique illustrated Old Testament from 7th-century North Africa shows the story of Jacob and Esau, in which these representations of Esau the hunter might reflect the archery equipment used by the settled peoples of North Africa. (*Ashburnham Pentateuch*, Bibliothèque Nationale, Nouv. Acq. Lat. 2334, 4. 25a, Paris, France)

Having served as a base for Muslim operations into Septimania and other parts of southern France, the city of Lerida in north-western Spain remained a fortress throughout most of its history. Today 18th-century ramparts surround the remains of the medieval cathedral. (Author's photograph)

version of the widespread repeated attack and withdrawal. Previous Byzantine sources recorded that tribes that possessed large numbers of camels used them as a form of barrier outside their tented encampments. Men on foot then defended the resulting living field fortification using their spears as pikes. Meanwhile the tribe's cavalry tried to hold high ground outside the perimeter, from here they would attack the enemy if the latter attacked the camp.

Lhodari, the king of the Alamans presides over an assembly of magnates to agree the text of *The Law of the Alamans*, in this early 9th-century manuscript. It is a primitive drawing highlighting the cultural differences between Alemania in southern Germany and the still largely Romanized Mediterranean regions farther south, though both had once formed part the Merovingian Frankish Kingdom. (*Breviarium Alarici*, Bibliothèque Nationale, Paris, France)

A third group contributed to the military potential of the westernmost provinces of the Umayyad Caliphate during the Poitiers campaign; the descendants of the Visigoths including those who, in AD 714, had accepted Islamic suzerainty over Narbonne. They initially included the sons of a previous Visigothic king, Witiza, who were guaranteed local autonomy. How much of the Visigothic military aristocracy of Septimania and the rest of the Iberian Peninsula still played an active role in AD 732 is unclear, though some clearly did so.

The defensive organization of Septimania had also been the same as that of the rest of the Visigothic Kingdom and would probably have been amongst its most militarized provinces. The late Visigothic army had been based upon the king's *comitatus* of personal followers, plus local levies controlled by the Visigothic nobility. The late 7th-century Visigothic senior aristocracy also had their own forces of *buccellarii*. There were, however, unlikely to have been any identifiably Germanic elements within late-Visigoth urban garrisons and the royal *comitatus* had been destroyed during the Arab-Berber conquest of AD 711–712. Some of the remaining troops could be absorbed as *mawalis*, and the *mawali* system would soon become a significant feature of early Andalusian military organization.

Amongst the varied objects in the so-called 'Lombard Treasure' is a small gold cross. Sometimes still regarded as a fake, it is nevertheless typical of the sort of embossed gold decoration that covered many sacred objects during the 7th and 8th centuries AD. (Private collection)

BELOW, TOP
This remarkable sword was found many years ago at Moussais-le-Bataille, close to the site of the battle of Poitiers, and is believed to have come from a grave of one or several Muslim warriors. The blade would be typical of that period but the hilt is so unusual that it might have been added after the sword was excavated (present whereabouts unknown)

BELOW, BOTTOM
The blade of a very early Islamic sword, traditionally said to have belonged to the Umayyad Caliph Umar II Ibn Abd al-Aziz, AD 717–720. (Topkapi Reliquary, Istanbul, Turkey)

The Muslim Army's camp featured prominently in accounts of the battle of Poitiers. The normal Arabic word for such a military encampment was *khandaq*, from the Persian *kanda* meaning a defensive ditch or trench. It had been used since the days of the Prophet Muhammad and was a common feature, ranging from a simple field fortification to a fully fortified base camp. In fact the *khandaq* became increasingly important in the later Umayyad period, and armies on the march often defended themselves with a *khandaq* every night. Abd al-Hamid Ibn Yahya, writing at the close of the Umayyad period, provided instructions for the construction of such a defence. After the baggage was set down and the troops were designated places to sleep, but before any tents were set up, each *qa'id* officer should be assigned a section of surrounding ground where his men must dig a trench. This should then be defended with *hasak*, meaning thorns or caltrops, and should have two entrances, each guarded by an officer with 100 men.

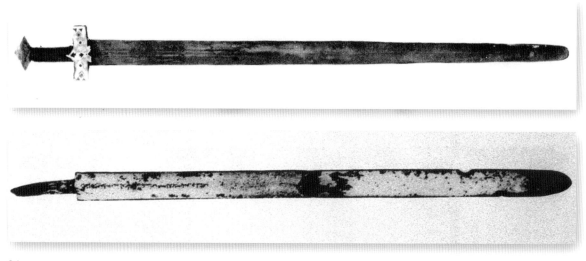

OPPOSING PLANS

CHRISTIAN PLANS

For Charles Martel, the Muslim incursion into the principality of Aquitaine, and from there towards Tours, threatened to destroy one of the Merovingian Kingdom's most sacred shrines and was a potential challenge to the integrity of the *Regnum Francorum* – the Frankish Kingdom. The church of Saint-Martin outside Tours was not only one of the greatest in Latin Christendom but the city of Tours was also a key position on the frontier between Frankish Neustria and the principality of Aquitaine, which the Merovingian state still claimed as part of the *Regnum Francorum*. There was, however, no evidence that the campaign was seen by any except some churchmen, as primarily being between Christianity and Islam. Charles Martel's plan was essentially very simple and reflected the strategic and tactical traditions with which he and his troops were familiar. Though primarily defensive, it would largely be fought within another state, the principality of Aquitaine.

It was traditional for Frankish armies to muster in spring, but this was for an offensive campaign. Charles Martel almost certainly knew that the Muslims were preparing an offensive and he therefore remained within

The Roc de Carroux leading to the Cerdagne region of the eastern Pyrenees is a broad but rugged plateau. It was in these mountains that the Berber frontier governor, Munusa, rose in rebellion against the Umayyad governors of al-Andalus. His Berber tribal followers might have felt at home here because the terrain and climate are similar to parts of the High Atlas Mountains in their native Morocco. (Author's photograph)

Virtually nothing remains of the mosaics that decorated some of the wealthiest churches of the Merovingian period, but they are likely to have been similar to this remarkable and only slightly later 9th-century mosaic in a church near Orléans. (*in situ*, Oratory of Germigny-des-Prés; author's photograph)

Merovingian territory until the direction of any such assault became clear. It is also important to note that, in the early medieval period, well-trained and properly equipped infantry enjoyed several advantages over men on horseback when their numbers were equivalent and the battlefield was suitable for relatively static, defensive tactics.

The Aquitainian plan was even more defensive and reactive. Some historians have maintained that Eudes had been seeking peace with the Muslims and some even suggested that he sought help from them in an attempt to take control of Neustria and perhaps Burgundy. If this was so, then Eudes' ambitions went sadly awry. In reality there is little or no evidence for such a scenario and the Umayyad governor of al-Andalus' decision to attack Aquitaine in AD 732 is the strongest evidence that it was a myth.

The campaign itself indicates that Prince Eudes initially feared a Muslim attack along the main road from Lerida, via the Cerdagne and Ariège towards Toulouse. This would have been the normal enemy approach and the high plateau of the Cerdagne, with its formidable *castella*, had been the key to Septimania and Aquitaine for centuries and would remain strategically vital until at least the 18th century. Munusa, the Berber rebel, had also held it, which was surely why Prince Eudes established marriage alliance with him. So Eudes may initially have assembled his army on the north-eastern bank of the Garonne from where he could defend Toulouse. If so, the Muslim assault across the western Pyrenees left him on the wrong side of river and perhaps uncertain whether there would be a second Muslim thrust from Narbonne. Such hesitation may have been why Eudes was slow to reassemble his forces close to the Dordogne from where he is said to have moved too late to save Bordeaux.

MUSLIM PLANS

Abd al-Rahman al-Ghafiqi's campaign of AD 732 was not intended to conquer France, still less to overrun Christian Europe. It was merely a *razzia* or raid, though a substantial one, and as such was within an established

Umayyad strategy of sending repeated small-scale attacks in which each army consisted only of what was necessary for its limited aim. Campaigns on other peripheral fronts, ranging from Central Asia to India and the Sudan, employed the same cautious category. Nevertheless, the Arabs lost their famous strategic mobility in mountains, marshy terrain and forested landscapes. They would clearly do so in AD 732.

Nevertheless, there is heated scholarly debate about the precise aim of this campaign. A. D. Taha, for example, maintains that the Umayyad governor of al-Andalus hoped to extend Islamic control into the northern slopes of the Pyrenees where he hoped to resettle some of the 'troublesome Berbers'. He notes as evidence, statements in some Christian sources that these Berbers brought their families with them. K. Blankinship, however, states: 'Even if settlement was eventually contemplated, it would never have been carried out on a long-distance raid that was the very first reconnoitring of the area'. Ibn Abd al-Hakam, writing just over a century after the event, added another twist by describing the northwards extension of Abd al-Rahman al-Ghafiqi's operation, beyond Poitiers towards the Merovingian Frankish Tours, as a separate campaign: 'He then led another military expedition against the Franks'. This view is repeated by several later Muslim sources.

Mountains proved significant barriers for armies burdened with siege equipment, and it is unlikely that al-Ghafiqi's large raiding force had such weaponry with them when they crossed the western Pyrenees. This would also have meant that they could only take significant fortified places by assault, through treason or by destroying the defending garrison in battle

BELOW LEFT
The military elites of those southern European regions which clung most firmly to their Roman heritage appear to have been dressed and equipped in a strange mixture of late Roman, Germanic and Byzantine styles. This is clearly illustrated on a mid-7th- to mid-8th-century wall painting in Rome, though the self-consciously 'Roman' military aristocracy of Aquitaine was probably similar. (*in situ* Church of Santa Maria Antiqua, Rome, Italy)

BELOW RIGHT
Some of the best-preserved wall paintings in the Umayyad reception hall at Qusayr Amra are high on the ceiling. They include huntsmen or warriors, one of whom is an infantry archer who draws his thick bow using two fingers rather than the thumb-drawn normally associated with such a weapon. (*in situ* Qusayr Amra, Jordan; author's photograph)

The massive fortress of Mont Louis was built to close the eastern end of a pass through the Pyrenees linking Spain and France. It has always been a strategically important route, the western or Spanish end of which was dominated by the castle of Llivia where the rebel Berber governor of the Cerdagne area had his capital. Today Llivia remains a Spanish enclave surrounded by French territory, a relic of the centuries when the two states struggled for control of this pass. (Author's photograph)

outside the walls. During the 8th century AD there were few usable passes across the Pyrenees – a handful being suitable for wagons in good weather, some being passable by mule trains, while most could only be used by men on foot. However, the greatest obstacles seem to have been the dense forests rather than the mountains themselves, particularly in the west where the Roncesvalles Pass ran through particularly dense and often rain-soaked woods. Meanwhile, the main routes were still the Roman roads from Pamplona to Dax via Saint-Jean-le-Vieux and Garris. Another route lay across the Ibañeta Pass.

Why, then, did the Umayyad *wali* ignore the easier eastern passes used by his predecessors in favour of the more difficult western ones? Why also did he neglect the Mediterranean coastal route where an army could be supported by a fleet? Perhaps political as well as strategic considerations were involved. According to Taha, the bulk of al-Ghafiqi's army were 'unreliable' Berbers who had settled in the Asturias and southern Pyrenean foothills, and that this was why he selected Pamplona as his military base. Taha also suggested that most of the Arab participants were from the Kalb tribal confederation that had settled around Saragossa and along the Ebro Valley. The recent rebellion by some northern Iberian Muslims led by Manusa may also have given the new Umayyad governor cause for concern. However, a more immediate reason for Abd al-Rahman al-Ghafiqi's strategy may have been the knowledge that Charles Martel currently threatened Prince Eudes of Aquitaine. Any consequent weakening of Eudes' forces would enable the raiders to press rapidly northwards while subsidiary raiding forces spread devastation farther afield.

THE CAMPAIGN

CRUSHING MUNUSA

Abd al-Rahman al-Ghafiqi started preparing for what became his Poitiers campaign almost immediately he became *wali* of al-Andalus in AD 730. Meanwhile Prince Eudes of Aquitaine had already formed an alliance with Munusa, the rebel Berber governor of the Cerdagne, an alliance supposedly cemented by the marriage of Munusa to Eudes' illegitimate daughter Lampégia. This the new *wali* presumably saw as a threat to his control over the only superficially Muslim Berbers in al-Andalus and more immediately to Umayyad rule in Septimania, al-Ghafiqi's previous governorate for which he probably felt special responsibility.

During those two years, Abd al-Rahman al-Ghafiqi toured al-Andalus, settling disputes, ensuring troops would be ready for the forthcoming campaign, and telling volunteers to assemble around Pamplona. In AD 731 many such volunteers arrived from North Africa, probably booty-hungry Berbers. Traditional though later and exaggerated accounts of the campaign state that volunteers came from the Atlas Mountains, the deserts of Africa, the banks of the Nile, Syria and Arabia, while many *Mozarabs*, Andalusian Christians, as well as Jews supposedly volunteered as infantry along with Christian mercenaries 'known for their bravery'. Some historians have estimated the resulting army to number from 15,000 to 20,000 fighters plus their families, though such a figure seems improbably high. Nevertheless, Abd al-Rahman al-Ghafiqi soon had a formidable, well-organized, highly motivated and confident force under his command.

According to some of the oldest written sources, the early Muslim Arabs knew about stirrups but for many year chose not to adopt them. One of the first Middle Eastern representations of primitive loop-stirrups lacking a rigid step appears on this 7th- or 8th-century textile from Egypt. (Inv. 11.18, Textile Museum, Washington, USA; author's photograph)

The idea that the troops were accompanied by their families and children, intending to settle in newly conquered land, appeared in Paul the Deacons's *History of the Lombards* written later in the 8th century AD, but this may have mixed up accounts of the failed siege of Toulouse in AD 721 and the Poitiers campaign 11 years later. It was, nevertheless, repeated in the Chronicle of *Sigebert of Gembloux* and in the later *Grandes Chroniques de Saint-Denys*, which added that they brought 'all their substance' and 'harness' in order to settle in France.

Charles Martel also feared the alliance between Eudes and Munusa and, more immediately, between Eudes and Charles' great rival for power in Merovingian Neustria, the ex-mayor of the palace, Rainfroi. Information gathering in 8th-century Western Europe was faster than is generally realized and Charles Martel is said to have learned of the Eudes–Manusa alliance

Islamic raids into France (Gaul) from AD 714 to 731

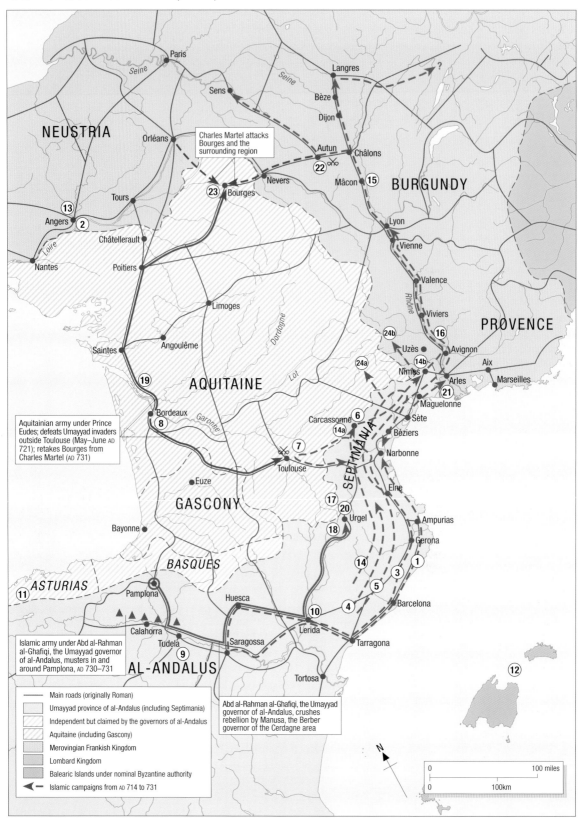

Charles Martel attacks Bourges and the surrounding region

Aquitainian army under Prince Eudes; defeats Umayyad invaders outside Toulouse (May–June AD 721); retakes Bourges from Charles Martel (AD 731)

Islamic army under Abd al-Rahman al-Ghafiqi, the Umayyad governor of al-Andalus, musters in and around Pamplona, AD 730–731

Abd al-Rahman al-Ghafiqi, the Umayyad governor of al-Andalus, crushes rebellion by Manusa, the Berber governor of the Cerdagne area

NEUSTRIA
BURGUNDY
PROVENCE
AQUITAINE
SEPTIMANIA
GASCONY
BASQUES
ASTURIAS
AL-ANDALUS

Paris
Sens
Langres
Bèze
Dijon
Orléans
Autun
Châlons
Mâcon
Nevers
Bourges
Tours
Angers
Châtellerault
Lyon
Vienne
Poitiers
Nantes
Limoges
Valence
Viviers
Saintes
Angoulême
Uzès
Avignon
Nîmes
Aix
Arles
Marseilles
Bordeaux
Maguelonne
Carcassonne
Sète
Béziers
Narbonne
Toulouse
Elne
Euze
Ampurias
Gerona
Bayonne
Urgel
Pamplona
Barcelona
Huesca
Calahorra
Lerida
Tarragona
Tudela
Saragossa
Tortosa

Seine
Loire
Dordogne
Lot
Garonne
Rhône

Main roads (originally Roman)

Umayyad province of al-Andalus (including Septimania)

Independent but claimed by the governors of al-Andalus

Aquitaine (including Gascony)

Merovingian Frankish Kingdom

Lombard Kingdom

Balearic Islands under nominal Byzantine authority

Islamic campaigns from AD 714 to 731

0   100 miles
0   100km

N

through his 'spies', though merchants, churchmen and pilgrims probably spread the news. In AD 731 a meeting between Eudes and Rainfroi caused Charles Martel more concern and so he exiled an influential supporter of Rainfroi, Abbot Wandon of Fontenelle, to Maastricht where he could be kept under close observation. Bishop Aimar of Auxerre was similarly imprisoned at Bastogne, perhaps for having helped Eudes, but these actions merely increased hostility to Charles and support for Rainfroi.

The threat posed by the Muslims seems to have been a secondary consideration for Charles Martel. Nevertheless, the year AD 731 also saw a 'Saracen' raid up the Rhône Valley against Burgundy, which was nominally under Frankish suzerainty. At the time Charles himself was in Neustria, gathering his considerable military forces but instead of helping Haimer of Auxerre, the governor of most of Burgundy, Charles Martel moved to Austrasia where he focused upon the military organization of the Franks' eastern frontier facing the pagan Saxons. This is further evidence that Charles Martel did not see the Muslims as a major threat.

In fact Muslim operations in and around the Rhône Valley were mere *razzias* to undermine local resistance and gather booty. For example, in the spring of AD 731 one such force was operating between the Rhône River and Cevennes Mountains, along a main road towards Lyon. The Muslims raided the areas around Uzès and Viviers, as well as the Valentinois and Viennois on the right bank of the Rhône. This or another force reached Lyon, Mâcon and Chalon, all of which they reportedly burned, though this may have referred to the suburbs rather than the fortified centres. According to near-hysterical Christian

Islamic raids into France (Gaul) from AD 714 to 731

1 Probable raid led by Tarik Ibn Ziyad, taking Barcelona and Narbonne where 'pro-Witiza' Visigothic nobles accept Umayyad overlordship in return for autonomy in Septimania (AD 714), supposedly also raiding 'towards Avignon and Lyon' (Visigoths of Septimania subsequently reassert their independence under King Ardo).

2 Rainfroi, ex-Mayor of the Neustrian Merovingian Palace and rival of Charles Martel, seeks refuge in Angers (AD 716).

3 Islamic raid under al-Hurr al-Thaqafi, the Umayyad governor of al-Andalus, into Catalonia and currently independent Septimania (AD 716–17).

4 Probable start of Islamic campaign of conquest north of the Pyrenees under al-Hurr al-Thaqafi, into Roussillon area (AD 718).

5 Islamic campaign led by al-Samh al-Khawlani, Umayyad governor of al-Andalus, takes Narbonne (AD 719) and overthrows the Visigothic King Ardo (perhaps overthrown the following year).

6 Governor al-Samh al-Khawlani continues his campaign, probable start of the prolonged siege of Carcassonne (AD 720).

7 Major thrust by Muslim army under Governor al-Samh al-Khawlani; siege of Carcassonne begun or intensified (March AD 721); Muslims also besiege Toulouse but are defeated by Prince Eudes of Aquitaine near the city, al-Samh being killed (11 May or 9/10 June AD 721); Muslim army withdraws to Narbonne under Abd al-Rahman al-Ghafiqi.

8 Rigobert, the ex-bishop of Rheims and supporter of Rainfroi (ex-Mayor of the Neustrian Merovingian Palace) is exiled by Charles Martel and seeks refuge with Prince Eudes (AD 721).

9 Fortunio, the Visigothic lord of the Borja district, converts to Islam and recognizes Umayyad overlordship (between AD 721 and 732).

10 Amrus, the Visigothic lord of the Lerida area, recognises Umayyad overlordship (between AD 721 and 732).

11 Don Pelayo (Pelagius), a Visigothic nobleman, defeats a local Islamic force in the Covadonga area, this being the traditional start of the Christian 'Reconquista' of the Iberian Peninsula (28 May AD 722).

12 Muslim fleet raids the Byzantine-ruled Balearic islands, as well as Byzantine Sardinia and Lombard Corsica (AD 724).

13 Rainfroi, ex-mayor of the Neustrian Merovingian palace, 'rebels' against Charles Martel (AD 724).

14 Anbasa Ibn Suhaym al-Kalbi, the Umayyad governor of al-Andalus, leads an army against Carcassonne, which has been under siege since c. AD 720 (14a) and Nîmes (14b), marking the definitive end of the Visigothic Kingdom (AD 725).

15 After taking Nîmes, Anbasa Ibn Suhaim the Umayyad governor of al-Andalus leads a raiding force up the Rhône Valley, temporarily taking Autun (22 August AD 725); Muslim raiders reach Sens, Luxeuil and Langres; the raiders might also have reached the Vosges Mountains east of Langres; they then withdraw to the southern part of the Rhône Valley (AD 725).

16 Unconfirmed raid sent by by Abd al-Rahman al-Ghafiqi, the current Umayyad governor of Septimania, towards Avignon, Viviers, Valence, Vienne and Lyon (AD 726).

17 Prince Eudes of Aquitaine reportedly gives his illegitimate daughter Lampégia, in marriage to Munusa, the Berber Muslim governor of the Cerdagne region, to cement an alliance (AD 729).

18 Munusa, the Berber governor of the Cerdagne area, rebels against the authority of the Umayyad governor of al-Andalus (between AD 729 and 731).

19 Rainfroi, ex-mayor of the Neustrian Merovingian palace, meets Prince Eudes which makes Charles Martel fear an alliance against himself; other exiles also encourage Eudes' hostility towards Charles Martel (AD 731).

20 Abd al-Rahman al-Ghafiqi, now the Umayyad governor of al-Andalus, crushes the rebellion by Munusa, governor of the Cerdagne area, taking the fortress of Llivia; Munusa commits suicide (AD 731).

21 The local governor of Septimania sends a raiding force against Arles (AD 731)

22 Local forces reportedly defeated by 'Saracen' raiders near Couches (22 August AD 731).

23 Two raids by Charles Martel take Bourges and ravage the Berry region; Prince Eudes immediately retakes Bourges (AD 731).

24a-b Undated and unconfirmed Muslim raids against Millau and Alès.

sources, men were slaughtered while women and children were dragged southwards as slaves; only those who hid in forests and mountains escaping.

The raiders then seem to have divided into two units; one continuing northwards along the Roman road towards Langres and reaching the area of Dijon where they destroyed the monastery of Bèze and possibly that of Saint-Seine. Here two monks, Altigianus and Hilarinus, were martyred on 23 August. Langres was so ruined that its church was still unrepaired 83 years later. The second group of raiders headed towards the wealthy city of Autun, which fell on 22 August and was similarly put to the torch. On the same day the raiders defeated a local force near Couches commanded by a local bishop named Emiland who was slain. Later declared a saint, this perhaps mythical churchman was remembered in the name of a local village, Saint-Emiland. This was also when Saint Frou abandoned the ruins of his monastery of Saint-Martin to become a hermit in the forests of Duemois.

Now the 'Saracens' headed for lower Burgundy, probably towards Saulieu and Avallon, passing close to Auxerre but then suddenly stopping near Sens. The bishop of that town, Saint Ebbon was a retired soldier who organized a local defence that reportedly defeated the raiders who therefore retreated. There may have been a clash in which the Muslims were worsted, but their withdrawal southwards is more likely to have been because they now had sufficient booty and captives. Otherwise there seems to have been no effective resistance in southern Burgundy, with Duke Haimer of Auxerre clearly being unable to stop these invaders. Nor did the mountains of Velay protect the ancient monastery of Calmeliacus whose bishop-abbot Chaffre was killed. Later canonized, his saint's day was 19 October, which may have been when he was martyred, in which case the raiders were still ravaging the region as they pulled back to Septimania.

Unclear later sources suggest that the Muslim garrisons of Septimania also attacked Arles around the same time that governor al-Ghafiqi crushed the rebel Munusa in AD 731, defeating local Christian defenders outside the walls but being unable to take fortified Arles itself. This may, in fact, have been to divert attention away from the possibility of an assault across the western Pyrenees.

Meanwhile, the year AD 731 saw Charles Martel's troops twice attack the north-eastern region of the principality of Aquitaine, probably as a warning

Oxen rather than horses were normally used as heavy draught animals in early medieval France, as shown here in a 9th-century, early Carolingian manuscript. Local armies would have needed such wagons and animals to carry their heavier equipment and supplies, though the invading Arabs and Berbers made greater use of camels. (*Folchard's Psalter*, Stiftsbibliothek, St Gallen. Cod. 23, p.12, Swtizerland)

rather than a serious effort to crush Eudes. Here the Franks crossed the Loire, seizing and plundering Bourges, the capital of Berry, though this was promptly retaken by Eudes. It seems that Charles used Prince Eudes' supposed breaking of a treaty signed in AD 720 and the Aquitainian ruler's alliance with Munusa as pretexts for the attack. This Frankish propaganda was later accepted as historical fact and did much to undermine the reputation Eudes had previously earned by defeating a major Muslim invasion outside Toulouse. Charles Martel was, of course, presenting himself to the pope as the primary defender of Christendom. Coincidentally, Pope Gregory II died that same year, to be succeeded by Gregory III who remained pope until AD 741, while Charles Martel's inveterate rival, Rainfroi, also died in AD 731.

Meanwhile to the south, Abd al-Rahman al-Ghafiqi was completing his preparations despite tensions that had developed between himself and his nominal superior, Ubayda Ibn Abd al-Rahman al-Sulami the wali of North Africa. Later sources mention: 'A piece of furniture inlaid with pecious metals and jewels that he [Abd al-Rahman] had captured but not forwarded, instead choosing to smash it up in order to divide it amongst his troops.'

The reality may have been a dispute over the sharing of a special gazu tax, raised before major expeditions.

Once al-Ghafiqi felt strong enough to crush Munusa, the rebel governor of the Cerdagne region, he launched what seems to have been a sudden attack that may have caught Munusa by surprise. The date of this important but barely recorded campaign is unclear but was probably the summer or early autumn of AD 731, though some sources claimed Munusa had been defeated before Abd al-Rahman al-Ghafiqi became *wali* of al-Andalus; perhaps recalling a previous and less decisive clash. The little that is known with reasonable certainty is that al-Ghafiqi invaded Munusa's fiefdom, defeated his troops, took his main fortress of Llivia and then cornered Munusa in the mountains where the rebel killed himself by leaping from a cliff. According to Isidore of Beja, Munusa was covered with wounds and abandoned by his allies, and so threw himself from high rocks near Puigcerda. Less reliable but more romantic accounts of the campaign claim that Munusa's wife, the fair Lampégia, was captured by al-Ghafiqi who supposedly sent her to join the Caliph Hisham's harem in Syria, accompanied by her late husband's head. Others maintain that Prince Eudes' daughter joined the Andalusian governor's household.

A form of sword hilt that evolved from Roman traditions persisted in the Islamic Middle East until the later medieval period. It was entirely different from that seen in early medieval Europe and is represented by this 8th- or 9th-century, Umayyad or early Abbasid sword-guard from the Muslim pilgrimage way station of al-Rabadhah in Arabia. (Archaeological Museum, King Sa'ud University, Riyadh, Saudi Arabia)

THE INVASION OF AQUITAINE

In May or early June AD 732, Abd al-Rahman al-Ghafiqi launched his main campaign against Aquitaine. The army assembled between the upper Ebro River and Pamplona, marched through that city and headed for the passes. Al-Ghafiqi and his main force went through the Roncesvalles Pass, the Bidassia (Bidouze) Valley and what are now the provinces of Bigorre and Comminges. The reasons for taking this difficult and potentially dangerous

The invasion of Aquitaine, spring and early summer AD 732

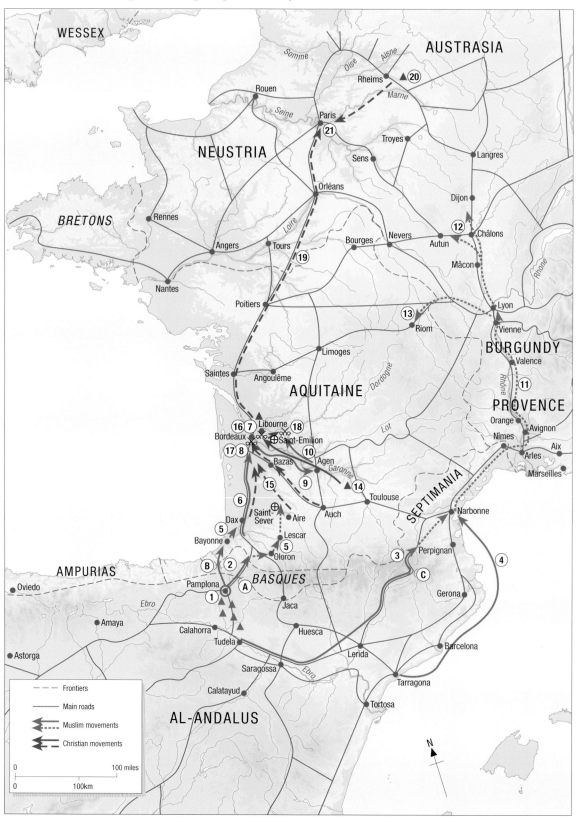

WESSEX

AUSTRASIA

Somme

Oise

Aisne

Rouen

Rheims

▲ 20

Seine

Marne

Paris

21

NEUSTRIA

Troyes

Sens

Langres

Orléans

Dijon

BRETONS

Rennes

Châlons

12

Angers

Tours

Bourges

Nevers

Autun

Mâcon

19

Rhône

Nantes

Poitiers

Lyon

13

Riom

Vienne

Limoges

BURGUNDY

Valence

Saintes

Angoulême

Dordogne

AQUITAINE

11

PROVENCE

Orange

Avignon

Libourne

18

Nîmes

Aix

16 7

Saint-Émilion

Arles

Bordeaux

10

Lot

Marseilles

17 8

Bazas

Agen

Garonne

15

14

SEPTIMANIA

9

Toulouse

Narbonne

6

Saint-

Dax

Sever

Aire

Auch

5

Lescar

3

Perpignan

Bayonne

5

4

B

Oloron

C

2

AMPURIAS

BASQUES

Gerona

Oviedo

Pamplona

A

1

Ebro

Jaca

Amaya

▲

Calahorra

Huesca

Astorga

Tudela

Lerida

Barcelona

Saragossa

Ebro

Tarragona

Calatayud

Tortosa

AL-ANDALUS

- - - Frontiers

—— Main roads

← Muslim movements

← Christian movements

0   100 miles

0   100km

N

The invasion of Aquitaine, spring and early summer AD 732

Muslim movements

1 Muslim army assembled in upper Ebro Valley, with Abd al-Rahman al-Ghafiqi's headquarters at Pamplona (winter and early spring).
2 Muslim main force crosses the Pyrenees through the Roncesvalles Pass (A), perhaps with a small force or the left 'wing' crossing via the Bidassia Valley (B) (May or June).
3 A smaller Muslim force supposedly crosses the Pyrenees via the Llivia Pass (C) into Septimania; perhaps as a diversionary attack, or to strengthen the garrisons in Septimania, or as the right 'wing' of the main force (late spring).
4 Muslim fleet supposedly sailing from Tarragona to Narbonne, perhaps with supplies and heavy equipment such as siege machinery, or to strengthen the Septimania garrisons (spring).
5 Muslim main force raids widely, ravaging Oloron, Lescar, Bayonne, and burning the abbey of Saint-Sever.
6 Muslim main force under Abd al-Rahman al-Ghafiqi heads for Bordeaux while separate raiding columns spread confusion and the rear forces mop up remaining enemy garrisons.
7 Muslim force, probably a separate raiding column, destroys the supposed monastery of Saint-Emilion north of the Garonne and defeats the 'Count of Libourne'.
8 Muslim main force defeats Prince Eudes south of Bordeaux (June?); Muslim main force takes Bordeaux, burns the churches and assembles enormous booty (June?).
9 Muslim force marches up the south bank of the Garonne and pillages Agen, followed by widespread raiding.
10 Muslim main force crosses the Garonne and defeats Prince Eudes near the junction of the rivers Garonne and Dordogne (July?).

11 Muslim raiders or a diversionary force are operating in Burgundy in support of the Duke of Burgundy's attempt to regain independence from the Merovingian Franks (spring?).
12 Muslim raiders reportedly attack the Autun area and sack Savigny.
13 Muslim raiders are operating in the Auvergne region near Riom (summer?).

Christian movements

14 Prince Eudes musters his army near the Garonne, probably in the southern region close to the frontiers (spring).
15 Christian local forces and 'Muslim allies' (perhaps remnants of Munusa's followers) are defeated; they evacuate Auch, Dax, Aire and Bazas (May–June).
16 The 'Count of Libourne' is defeated and executed by the Muslims after the latter destroy the supposed monastery of Saint-Emilion.
17 Prince Eudes chooses battle outside Bordeaux, presumably south of the city to avoid being trapped in Bordeaux or in the Medoc Peninsula, but is defeated (June); the garrison of Bordeaux abandons the city.
18 Prince Eudes reassembles his troops (including the Bordeaux garrison?) near the junction of the Garonne and Dordogne rivers, but is again defeated (July?).
19 Prince Eudes heads for Reims to warn Charles Martel of the invasion and ask for support, perhaps meeting Charles Martel near Paris.
20 Charles Martel in Reims, presumably to watch in case of another major Muslim raid up the Rhône Valley, now receives news of the invasion of Aquitaine and heads for Paris.
21 Charles Martel issues a 'general ban' to raise a large army (summer).

route are unrecorded but by doing so he avoided Toulouse where one of his predecessors came to grief. Unlike his Visigothic predecessor, King Wamba, there is no evidence that al-Ghafiqi had to fight his way through Basque territory, which strongly suggests careful, but unrecorded, diplomatic preparations or that the Basques had been cowed by the crushing of Munusa. Other units probably used neighbouring passes, all of which led into Gascony in the south-western corner of the principality of Aquitaine. The fact that Gascony was also the heartland of Prince Eudes' power may have been a strategic consideration.

The idea put forward by some modern historians that al-Ghafiqi did not trust the garrisons of Septimania seems unlikely as he himself had recently been a highly effective governor of that province. He may, however, have been nervous about placing the Berber rebel Munusa's recent fiefdom on his vulnerable flank. It has also been suggested that, when the main Muslim force crossed the Pyrenees via the Roncesvalles Pass, a Muslim fleet went by sea from Taragona to Narbonne. If true, this may have carried the siege equipment which, under the conditions of the time, an army using the mountain passes would almost certainly have lacked. Even more tenuous evidence hints at a separate force crossing the mountains via the Cerdagne or Catalonia and Septimania into south-eastern Aquitaine. The fact that the destruction inflicted north of the Pyrenees was so widespread, and included supposedly fortified places, could indicate that the Muslims invaded by several routes and possessed at least some siege equipment.

Once they got through the mountains, al-Ghafiqi's forces ranged far and wide, ruthlessly demonstrating that their commander did not regard Prince Eudes as an ally. Muslim columns devastated Oloron, Lescar and Bayonne while abbeys were reportedly burned. On the other hand, doubt has been cast upon the destruction of monasteries in Pyrenean Gascony for the simple reason that this region was not as yet Christian. Records of comparable

In AD 732 Abd al-Rahman al-Ghafiqi led his army across the western Pyrenees from Pamplona into Aquitaine, the first time a large Muslim force had used this route. His main force went through the Roncesvalles Pass in Basque territory, which was notably wetter and more densely forested than the passes through the eastern Pyrenees. (Author's photograph)

A carpenter at work on a roof, in an early 9th-century Frankish manuscript. Such workmen played a vital role in the armies of the Merovingian and early Carolingian periods, erecting fortifications and demolishing those of the enemy. (*Canon Tables of the Gospel Book of Ebbo*, Bibliothèque Municipale, Ms. 1, f.13, Épernay, France)

destruction in lowlands farther north are more trustworthy, including that of the abbeys of Saint-Savin-de-Lavedan and Saint-Sever-de-Rustan in *Gallia Christiana*. More surprising, perhaps, is the fact that the raiders met no serious resistance across the huge area between the Pyrenees and the river Garonne. Here separate columns advanced north, spreading destruction far afield as Abd al-Rahman al-Ghafiqi and his main force headed for Bordeaux. Prince Eudes is said to have had Berber allies in the mountains, presumably remnants of Manusa's failed rebellion. But these, and his own garrisons, fled towards the Garonne. Auch, Dax, Aire-sur-Adour and Bazas were abandoned then burned by the invaders while the Muslim rearguard supposedly mopped up residual resistance.

News of the Muslim eruption from the Pyrenees must have reached Prince Eudes quickly. Nevertheless, his movements remain unclear though it seems likely that, having mobilized the Gascons and the Basque 'militia', his troops remained close to the river Garonne, probably on its right bank. It is similarly unclear how many times Prince Eudes and his main army faced al-Ghafiqi in battle. Eudes' primary concern was to defend his capital city of Bordeaux but he also feared being trapped in the Medoc Peninsula, on a spit of land extending northwards from Bordeaux between the Gironde Estuary and the sea. One of the few near contemporary sources to describe these events is *The Mozarabic Chronicle* of AD 754, which merely mentioned a battle of Bordeaux and claimed that Aquitainian casualties were so high that 'only God knows how many died and [simply] vanished'. Apparently Prince Eudes had to choose between resisting inside Bordeaux and perhaps being trapped there, or fighting in the open outside. Perhaps recalling his victory outside Toulouse 11 years earlier, Eudes decided on the latter and so arrayed his troops somewhere 'beyond the gates of Bordeaux' where they were nevertheless defeated. The fact that he and a perhaps substantial part of his army escaped to fight on elsewhere strongly suggests that this, the first main battle of the campaign, took place near a point where the Garonne was narrow enough to cross with ease. The Muslim Army now entered

A simple drawing of two confronted armies in a late 8th- or 9th-century Carolingian manuscript. Infantrymen head both, but the artist has made a clear distinction between the apparently unarmed horsemen on the right, with their shoes and short tunics, and the mounted spearmen on the left with their bare feet and long tunics. (*The Trier Apocalypse*, Stadtbibliothek, Trier, Germany)

Bordeaux some time in June, burning the churches and perhaps much of the old Roman city, killing many citizens and gathering substantial loot. The city's governor, whom the invaders initially thought to be Prince Eudes, was reportedly executed.

Quite when the Muslims attacked Agen is again unclear. Nor is it certain that al-Ghafiqi's main force was involved, nor who was in command on the Aquitainian side though this may have been a second defeat for Eudes. The strongest evidence indicates that Prince Eudes reached the river Dordogne, which joins the Garonne north of Bordeaux, on the day he was defeated outside the city. There he assembled new troops plus stragglers from Bordeaux while Abd al-Rahman al-Ghafiqi marched along the southern bank of the Garonne to pillage Agen and, perhaps, to defeat Eudes for a second time. A more likely scenario is that only its existing garrison defended Agen and, having crossed the river to take the town, al-Ghafiqi marched back down the Garonne, his main force heading towards the confluence with the Dordogne.

It was here that Prince Eudes suffered a decisive defeat. The Aquitainians are believed to have been drawn up on the northern side of the Dordogne, probably defending a Roman bridge or ford on the main route towards Saintes, close to present-day Saint-André. However, even the broad Dordogne did not stop the furious Muslim assault and Prince Eudes' army fled, leaving the Aquitainian ruler with relatively few followers though these would surely have been his elite personal *comitatus*. Mention of fighting in which a 'Count of Libourne' was captured might indicate that the Muslims crossed the Dordogne several kilometres upstream, thus outflanking Prince Eudes' position. The Count of Libourne's wealth was reportedly distributed among al-Ghafiqi's troops and it is reasonably certain that neighbouring Saint-Emilion was also pillaged though it is unclear what actually existed here at that time; the first reference to a proper abbey dating from around 1110.

What is clear is that Eudes, with no realistic hope of saving his principality from further devastation, led his remaining followers northwards, heading for the Merovingian Frankish city of Reims where he hoped to ask an old enemy but fellow Christian, Charles Martel, for help. Some sources suggest they met in or near Paris, which might indicate that Charles travelled some way to meet Eudes. We know nothing of the details of what they agreed but Charles Martel promptly issued a general *ban* or military summons in order to raise the largest army possible. The speed with which he acted was typical and the force thus

The Pyrenean passes are often closed in winter, and even in April the weather can close in suddenly with unexpected consequences, as the author found while crossing the Pas de la Casa in Andorra. Small wonder that Abd al-Rahman al-Ghafiqi did not march his men across the mountains until May or June. (Author's photograph)

raised included large numbers of Austrasians and Burgundians, as well as the Neustrians whose territory was most immediately threatened.

Neither Charles Martel nor Eudes can have known Abd al-Rahman al-Ghafiqi's plans, so these preparations are likely to have been precautionary. But as soon as sufficient troops had been mustered, Charles Martel led his army to Orléans where he crossed the Loire before marching via Ambroise to the powerful frontier city of Tours. This he found undamaged though, given the rapidity of the Muslims' previous movements, he might have feared it would already be under threat.

For many years there has been heated debate about the precise location of the main battle between Charles Martel and Abd al-Rahman al-Ghafiqi. In a recent book on the subject, the French historian A-R. Voisin assembled a great deal of detailed evidence which he believed proves that the battle took place a few kilometres from Tours, at a place now called Ballan-Miré in an area called the Landes de Charlemagne. This, Voisin suggested, was originally named after Charles Martel rather than his grandson Charlemagne.

Although such an interpretation does not have to be accepted in full, it does seem likely that Charles Martel's army established its camp here, in a position ideally placed to protect the vulnerable basilica of Saint-Martin outside the fortified walls of Tours. From here they could also patrol the southern road along which the Muslims would advance. There may actually have been skirmishes between scouting or raiding parties not far from Ballan-Miré, but Charles Martel probably did not march south until al-Ghafiqi's outriders actually invaded Merovingian territory.

THE MUSLIMS MARCH NORTH

Having decisively defeated the Aquitainians, the Muslim Army spent the next three months raiding far and wide, assembling an astonishing volume of loot and facing no reported resistance. Saintes, Perigueux and Angoulême were all sacked, after which al-Ghafiqi reassembled his forces, probably at Saintes, and continued his march northwards. This took him along the old Roman Via I across relatively poor, and in many areas forested, land towards the famously rich abbey of Saint-Hilaire outside Poitiers. The presence of such large churches outside city walls was a common feature of this period, that at Saintes having almost certainly already being sacked. The *Annals of Aniane* and the *Chronicle of Fredegar* both describe such depredations while *The Mozarabic Chronicle* of AD 754 stated that the Muslims specifically destroyed 'palaces', probably meaning rural fortifications.

Poitiers had expanded since the old Roman city wall had been built, a larger area having been surrounded by a wall under Visigothic rule. Even so, the city did not reach the narrow but steep gorge of the river Boivre to the west and was significantly smaller than the later medieval city. At the same time there was plenty of evidence of building during the Merovingian period, most notably of the baptistry of Saint-Jean. There were substantial suburbs outside the walls while the fortifications now enclosed 40 to 42 hectares, making Poitiers the second biggest city in the principality of Aquitaine after Toulouse, bigger that the capital Bordeaux.

Poitiers' importance rested upon its location at a major road junction and a crossing over a navigable river. It was also a significant religious and economic centre, the great church of Saint-Hilaire having originally been built in the late Roman period. Restored early in the 6th century AD, it had been decorated with gold mosaic by the Frankish King Clovis and now contained several important religious and secular tombs. The unfortified quarter or suburb, which grew up around it from the 6th century AD onwards, was known as the *vicus* of Poitiers. Close to the western wall of Poitiers itself was a major Merovingian (and subsequently Carolingian) cemetery with another large church. A funerary basilica had similarly been constructed between the eastern city wall and the river Clain. Originally dedicated to the Virgin Mary, it came to be known as Saint-Radegonde and had been enlarged during the 7th century AD. Most of Poitiers' urban expansion was, in fact, on this eastern side between the city proper and the Clain. What is certain is that 8th-century Poitiers was not just a Roman relic and sacred site, but was a real city that included 'palaces'.

After sacking and looting the abbey-church of Saint-Hilaire and its suburb, the Muslim army did not try to take the strongly defended city of Poitiers. Despite the difficulty of passing so close to its formidable walls and

PRINCE EUDES MEETS CHARLES MARTEL, THE MEROVINGIAN MAYOR OF THE PALACE (pp. 50-51)

Following his defeats by the Muslims outside Bordeaux and next to the river Garonne, Prince Eudes of Aquitaine **(1)** went to his old enemy, Charles Martel **(2)** to ask for help against the invaders and to warn him of the threat they might pose to the Merovingian province of Neustria. The two leaders are said to have met near Paris, perhaps at one of the fortified timber villages **(3)** that the originally Germanic Franks had built across much of what are now the Low Countries and northern France. Subsequent events suggest that Eudes still had part of the Aquitainian Army under his command, probably the elite forces of his personal *comitatus* **(4)**. This probably looked rather different to Charles Martel's largely Frankish troops **(5)** because the Aquitainians were recruited from Basque tribesmen from the Pyrenees **(6)** and Gascons **(7)**, whose military traditions were a direct inheritance from the late Roman army.

towers, and of leaving a strong enemy-held city to his rear, Abd al-Rahman al-Ghafiqi decided to continue northwards towards the even richer abbey-church of Saint-Martin outside Tours. The fact that this was also one of the most significant Christian centres or, as an 8th-century Muslim would have seen it, a major centre of 'polytheism', may also have encouraged his army in this hazardous move. Tours, however, lay in Merovingian Frankish rather than Aquitainian territory and Abd al-Rahman al-Ghafiqi would be invading another very powerful kingdom.

The urban developments described above had left a relatively narrow corridor where the Roman road probably ran through characteristic extra-mural market gardens and past small farmsteads between Poitiers' fortifications and the Boivre Gorge. This was almost certainly the route taken by al-Ghafiqi's army. An alternative interpretation, preferred by some historians, suggests that the Muslims crossed the Boivre shortly before Poitiers and then took another Roman road towards Saumur, via Loudun, though this seems unlikely given subsequent events. The idea that the *shuhada*

One of the most remarkable wall paintings in the early 8th-century Umayyad reception hall at Qusayr Amra shows a hunting scene. Horsemen and men on foot with burning brands chase wild animals into an area surrounded by netting. Outside this netting, at the bottom of the painted panel, is a tent almost identical in shape to those still used by the bedouin of Jordan and the neighbouring Arab countries. (*in situ* Qusayr Amra, Jordan; author's photograph)

Another of the often-ignored wall paintings on the ceiling of the Umayyad reception hall at Qusayr Amra shows a horseman with a spear which he thrusts at an animal on the ground. Though based upon Christian religious iconography, the man himself wears a bulky headcloth or turban, a flowing cloak, and does not use stirrups. (*in situ* Qusayr Amra, Jordan; author's photograph)

53

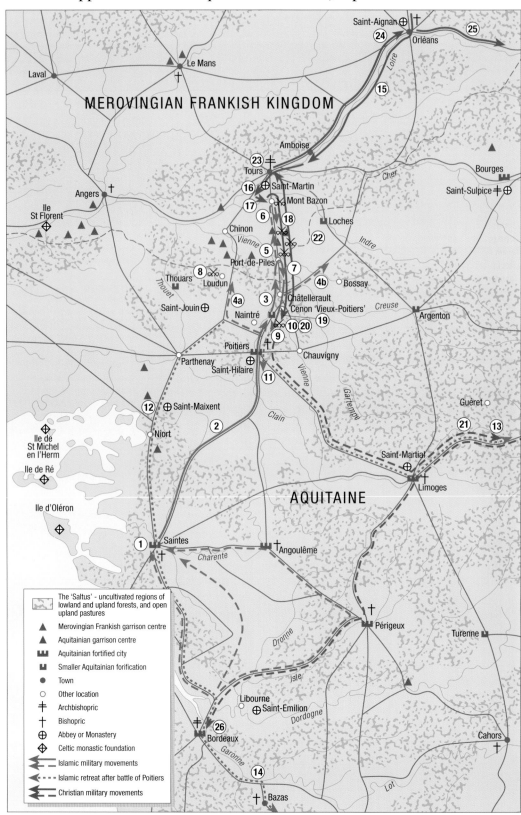

The 'Saltus' - uncultivated regions of lowland and upland forests, and open upland pastures

▲ Merovingian Frankish garrison centre

▲ Aquitainian garrison centre

Aquitainian fortified city

Smaller Aquitainian forification

● Town

○ Other location

✛ Archbishopric

✝ Bishopric

⊕ Abbey or Monastery

✛ Celtic monastic foundation

Islamic military movements

Islamic retreat after battle of Poitiers

Christian military movements

The final approach and subsequent withdrawals, September–October AD 732

Islamic movements

1. After several months pillaging and devastating the Bordeaux region, including Périgeux, Angoulême and Saintes, the Muslim Army reassembles (September).
2. Abd al-Rahman al-Ghafiqi leads the Muslim main force north from Saintes towards Poitiers where it sacks the abbey of Sainte-Hilaire but does not attack the fortified and strongly defended city, instead passing between Poitiers and the valley of the river Boivre.
3. Main Muslim army heads towards Tours, crossing the river Vienne at Cenon (late September).
4a–b. Possible Muslim flanking forces operating west around Loudun and perhaps also eastwards in the area north of Bossay.
5. Muslim advance-guard or vanguard crosses the river Creuse at Port-de-Piles; scouts or foragers attack a group of Christian pilgrims at Civray-sur-Esves, two of whom are subsequently proclaimed martyrs as Sts. Gratien and Aventinus; another possible skirmish near the so-called 'menhir des Arabes' prehistoric standing stone just south of Sainte-Maur.
6. Muslim scouts or advance-guard clashes with the Christian advance guard between the rivers Indre and Creuse, probably between Ballan-Miré and a location later known as Sainte-Catherine-de-Fierbois, and are forced to withdraw.
7. Muslim vanguard or main force attacks the Christian position at Port-de-Piles but is unable to cross the river Creuse (early October).
8. Probable clash near Niré, west of the rivers Clain and Vienne, between Muslim and Christian flanking forces (14 or 15 October).
9. Muslim main force either pulls back to, or advances no farther than, the river Vienne, and establishes a fortified camp between the rivers Vienne and Clain (18 October).
10. Battle of Poitiers (25 October); Abd al-Rahman al-Ghafiqi is killed, probably while defending the camp; the name of his successor is unknown and there may have been a division or collapse of command. His successor as governor of al-Andalus, Abd al-Malik Ibn Qatan al-Fihri, was currently in Ifriqiya (Tunisia) from where he led a naval raid against Byzantine-ruled Sicily during this same year, AD 732.
11. The Muslim Army withdraws in good order but leaves its booty and prisoners behind in order to slow any pursuit, then makes a temporary camp near Poitiers, probably south of the city (night of 25–26 October).
12. A separate group of Muslim troops, either from the left flank operating west of the main force or resulting from a division of command following the death of Abd al-Rahman al-Ghafiqi, make camp on wooded heights overlooking a Roman road in Deux-Sèvres.
13. The Muslim main force withdraws towards other Muslim forces operating in the Rhône Valley, via the abbey of Guéret, which was not attacked, and from there to Narbonne.
14. A separate group of retreating Muslim troops apparently withdraws along the route used by the invaders earlier in the year, but has to fight its way across the Pyrenees in the Bigorre region.

Christian movements

15. Having assembled a very large army at Orléans, Charles Martel crosses the river Loire, probably accompanied by Prince Eudes with his remaining troops, and marches along the southern bank of the river Loire, past Amboise towards Tours (September).
16. The Christian Army makes camp near Tours, probably at Ballan-Miré south-west of the city in order to protect the abbey of Saint-Martin.
17. Charles Martel defeats or forces back Muslim scouts or advance-guard between the rivers Indre and Creuse, then reportedly donates a sword to the chapel of Sainte-Catherine-de-Fierbois; this sword was supposedly given to Joan of Arc in the 15th century (early October).
18. The Christian Army marches south towards Poitiers, probably making camp facing Port-de-Piles on the north bank of the river Creuse, then advances to the west bank of the river Vienne, facing Cenon.
19. The Christian Army crosses the river Vienne and establishes a camp at or around the partially abandoned Roman *mansio* now known as Vieux-Poitiers (between 18 and 24 October).
20. Battle of Poitiers (25 October).
21. Prince Eudes and his Aquitainians pursue the retreating Muslim main force via Guéret, harrying the stragglers.
22. The Aquitainians are also apparently responsible for clearing enemy stragglers from the area between Poitiers, Bossay and Tours.
23. Charles Martel and his army return to Tours where he deprives the bishop of his temporal power as a local lord.
24. Charles Martel and his army return to Orléans where he expels and exiles Bishop Eucher who is replaced as local governor by a Frankish count.
25. Charles Martel and his army march to Auxerre where he expels and exiles Bishop Ainmar who is replaced as local governor by a Frankish count.
26. Prince Eudes returns to the devastated city and region of Bordeaux.

or 'martyrs' mentioned in some Arabic accounts of the resulting battles was a reference to the huge Gallo-Roman *martyrium* or cemetery near the Roman road outside Poitiers is even more unlikely as the bulk of those buried there were pagans – not even Christians and certainly not Muslims.

Whatever route the invaders took, it seems unlikely that the main body of the army reached Tours, though its scouts and perhaps even the advance guard may almost have done so. The most convincing interpretation, based upon admittedly inadequate original information, is that the Muslims marched beyond Poitiers along what was still a major Roman road, skirting the great forest of Moulière with the valley of the river Clain immediately to their left, then crossing the Vienne and following its course with the river again on their right. The only man-made obstacles would have been the Roman *mansio* at what is now called Vieux-Poitiers and the large village of Cenon where the Muslim Army would have crossed the river Vienne – itself a major and potentially hazardous undertaking.

How far north al-Ghafiqi's main force reached is one of the most tantalizing questions in the whole obscure history of the Poitiers campaign. The scattered and inadequate evidence seems to indicate that it crossed the Vienne without meeting serious opposition and, at some unclear date, reached

The sophistication of the military technology inherited by the Muslim Arabs when they conquered the Sassanian Empire in Iran is nowhere better demonstrated than in this 7th-century, late Sassanian or early Islamic iron gauntlet for a very heavily armoured cavalryman. (Inv. no. O.38824, Römisch-Germanisches Zentralmuseum, Mainz, Germany)

the river Creuse at what is now Port-de-Piles, just east of the confluence of the Creuse and Vienne. The old road had already moved away from the Vienne and, from then on, headed across the relatively open plateau of Sainte-Maure-de-Touraine towards Tours. Given current Umayyad military practice, there would have been flanking units, an advance guard and a rearguard at some distance from the main body in such open terrain. There were also likely to have been subsidiary raiding forces, perhaps ranging eastwards as far as the Bossay area and westwards, on the other side of the Vienne around Loudun. One such unit attacked a band of pilgrims on their way to Rome at Civray-sur-Esves, 10km east of the main road. The pilgrims included Gratien and Aventinus who were killed and later canonized as saints, Saint Gratien initially being buried at Civray though his body was later moved.

Certain military historians suggest that Charles Martel barred the passage of the Vienne at Cenon and also established himself on the right bank of the Creuse facing Port-de-Piles, but this was probably several days later and almost certainly in the reverse order. The *Grandes Chroniques de Saint-Denys* also maintained that the Muslims attacked the church of Saint-Martin outside Tours, far to the rear of these positions. During the 19th century there was, however, a local tradition that Muslims and Christians fought near Saint-Martin-le-Bel, about 'three leagues from Tours' in the forested Landes de Charlemagne. Others suggest that the first clash between Charles Martel's men and the advancing Muslims was on 11 October. Once again the most satisfactory interpretation of the evidence is that Muslim scouts or the advance guard found the Frankish position south of Tours to be strongly defended and so pulled back. Al-Ghafiqi may still have been some way south of the Creuse when he received this information and his main force had clearly not crossed that river, nor indeed yet reached the frontier between the principality of Aquitaine and Merovingian Neustria.

On the other hand, the advance forces of both armies clashed on more than one occasion, perhaps near Ballan-Miré and the Landes de Charlemagne, perhaps near a prehistoric standing stone now known as the *menhir des Arabes* just south of the village of Sainte-Maure, and almost certainly near the village of Sainte-Catherine-de-Fierbois. The latter clash seems to be recalled in a later legend associated with Jeanne d'Arc, who is said to have been given a votive sword that Charles Martel donated to the chapel of Sainte-Catherine after his victory. This clash may, in fact, be seen as marking Charles Martel's first move southwards from his camp outside Tours.

The most commonly accepted version of the battle of Poitiers has Charles Martel hurrying south until he met Abd al-Rahman al-Ghafiqi on the Roman road some 20km north-east of Poitiers, whereupon there was a prolonged stand-off before a decisive battle. The reality was more complicated. Charles Martel may now have hurried to bar the passage of the Creuse facing Port-de-Piles. Some time during the second week of October a substantial Muslim force probably attempted to cross that river but failed. Here, as at the crossing

Oloron-Sainte-Marie in the foothills of the Pyrenees, west of the Roncesvalles Pass, was one of the places sacked by the Muslim invaders when they entered Aquitaine in spring AD 732 . Whether a church was also destroyed is less clear, as the Basque inhabitants of this area were still largely pagan at the time. (Author's collection)

The Umayyad period was one of significant military and technological change, not least in the widespread adoption of stirrups by cavalrymen. Here a broken piece of stucco statuary from a palace complex built for the Caliph Hisham at Khirbat al-Mafjir in Palestine, clearly shows stirrup-leathers emerging from between the saddle-flaps towards the rider's foot. Like so much at Khirbat al-Mafjir it reflects an increasingly strong influence from eastern Iran and from Central Asia. (Rockefeller Museum, Jerusalem)

of the Vienne, the lie of the land was in favour of those defending the north bank where Charles Martel would have had ample space to deploy his troops without abandoning the crossing point whereas those attacking from the south bank were confined within a neck of land between the rivers.

Al-Ghafiqi's main force now pulled back across the Vienne, if they had crossed it in the first place, and established a defensive position between the Vienne and the Clain on or before 18 October. Charles Martel's army continued its advance through Port-de-Piles, Ingrandes and what is now Châtellerault to the river Vienne facing Cenon. L. Levillain and C. Samaran suggested that, during this period, the ruins now know as Vieux-Poitiers were almost as important as the city of Poitiers. This may be exaggerated, and the

THE MUSLIM ARMY BYPASSES POITIERS AND MARCHES TOWARDS TOURS (pp. 58-59)

After pillaging and burning the basilica of Saint-Hilaire **(1)**, Abd al-Rahman al-Ghafiqi, the *wali* or governor of the westernmost Umayyad province of al-Andalus **(2)**, led his army northwards intending to pillage the even wealthier church of Saint-Martin outside Tours. This meant that the Muslim force had to pass between the fortification of Poitiers **(3)** and the steep gorge of the river Boivre (to the right of this picture), following a Roman road which is understood to have been maintained in good condition long after the fall of the western half of the Roman Empire **(4)**. Al-Ghafiqi's army consisted of a core of professional Umayyad troops **(5)**, most of whom would have been Arabs,

plus *mawalis* (literally 'clients') most of whom would have been of Berber origin in this part of the Umayyad Caliphate **(6)**, though perhaps including Persians **(7)** and even some Turkish adventurers **(8)**. Meanwhile the bulk of the army consisted of ill-disciplined and very poorly equipped Berber tribesmen **(9)**, many of whom are said to have brought their families with them. On the march, however, the high standards of Umayyad military discipline would probably have been imposed, especially while passing so close to Poitiers, with flanking guards **(10)** as well as scouts, an advance guard and a rearguard protecting the baggage train **(11)**.

A fully armoured Frankish horseman wearing an apparently long-sleeved mail hauberk and pointed helmet, plus spear and shield, but still not using stirrups. It comes from a religious manuscript made in France in the late 8th century AD. (*Gellone Sacramentary*, Bibliothèque Nationale, Ms. Lat. 12048, Paris, France)

results of more recent archaeological investigations are yet to be published, but if this was the locality then called *Vetus Pictavis* it was certainly more than a heap of Roman ruins. Only ten years after the battle of Poitiers, the joint Frankish mayors of the palace, Carloman and Pepin the Short, divided the kingdom here. Just a century later, the Carolingian Emperor Charles the Bald similarly signed one of his imperial diplomas here. So it is unlikely that the site and its substantial Roman theatre failed to play some part in the upcoming confrontation.

Then there is the contentious issue of military operations in the rolling countryside west of the Vienne and Clain valleys. Without necessarily accepting the idea that the main operations were in this area, the evidence does suggest that substantial forces, either the flanking units of both armies or a large Muslim raiding unit, were active here. This would have been fully within Umayyad tactical traditions, and such movements perhaps formed part of the probing and manoeuvring that filled the next few days. There is also strong but inconclusive evidence of a significant clash on 11, 14 or 15 October near Loudun, *c.*40km west of the rivers. An autonomous Muslim mounted force may even have established an encampment here, and the overrunning of these field fortifications by part of the Frankish Army may have been recorded as the '*Pucna [Pugna]* of Nirac' on 11 October. The name Nirac might stem from the Gallo-Roman *Nintriacum* or *Niracum*, and there are now four locations called Niré around Loudun: Niré-le-Haut, Niré-le-Bas, Niré-des-Landes and Niré-le-Dolent, the latter perhaps recalling a necropolis for the dead of such a battle. Other local sources note a place

The Roman walls and towers of Dax in Gascony were maintained, strengthened and occasionally rebuilt throughout the medieval period. Their lower part survives in some areas, though they would originally have been much taller. Even so, Dax fell with apparent ease to the invading Muslims in AD 732. (Author's photograph)

'Meeting of Joab and Abner at the Pool of Gibeon', in a 9th-century Carolingian ivory book cover. This very fine carving includes such strongly late Roman influences that it seems likely to have come from one of the more Romanized southern provinces of the Carolingian state, such as Aquitaine, Provence or northern Italy. (Location unknown)

called Fontaine Sarrasine near Moulins in Deux-Sèvres, in the canton of Châtillon-sur-Sèvres, and a tradition that after the campaign bands of 'Saracens' who had been operating in the area of Neuville now settled as free men. If true, this is more likely to recall events after al-Ghafiqi's defeat.

The little village of Maubec is one of the few places in south-western France where early medieval rather than repaired Roman fortifications survive. They are very simple and cannot have caused much difficulty to the Muslims who ravaged the area in AD 732. (Author's photograph)

THE BATTLE OF POITIERS

Whatever was happening to the west, the main event was approaching its culmination between the Clain and Vienne. All sources agree that the first main clash took place on and alongside a major Roman road, and that both armies were large, though in the case of the Muslims these numbers included numerous camp followers. It is also clear that there was a period of stand-off before the battle. Other features were the Muslims' use of their standard tactic of adopting a strong defensive position and awaiting an enemy assault before a planned counterattack, and the Christians being hesitant about crossing the Vienne in the presence of a strong enemy but perhaps unaware of the Umayyad Army's traditionally defensive tactics.

Several different dates have been suggested for the main battle, and this probably reflects seven or eight days of preliminary skirmishing and manoeuvring. The crossing of the Vienne at Cenon would have been a major undertaking and so it is likely that the main armies camped on opposite banks for several days, each unwilling to attack, until Charles Martel made his move between 18 and 25 October. His troops got over the Vienne without hindrance before establishing a defensive position, almost certainly north of what is now the hamlet of Moussais-le-Bataille, probably in and around the

The early 8th-century Umayyad paintings on the walls and 'throne room' at Qusayr Amra are not only better known than those on the ceiling but illustrate military figures in greater detail, though they are also more damaged. Those on the right side of the throne room include two guardsmen with long spears who might represent Umayyad cavalry. (*in situ* Qusayr Amra, Jordan; author's photograph)

ex-Roman *mansio* at Vieux-Poitiers. Whether the Muslims made any attempt to defend this location is unknown; perhaps it was still held by a Christian garrison who had held out in the rear of the initial Muslim advance.

Given existing Muslim military traditions, it seems likely that al-Ghafiqi would have launched his first attack or counterattack before the Christian position was fully established, perhaps as they arrived at Vieux-Poitiers. Christian sources clearly state that the main battle took place on a Saturday during October AD 732. These fell on the 4th, 11th, 18th and 25th of the month, while Muslim sources record that Abd al-Rahman al-Ghafiqi died on 25 October during or as a result of the fighting. So that is virtually certainly the correct date for the main clash though fighting continued until the 31st, presumably during the Muslim retreat.

Information about the course of the battle is not only limited but is mostly couched in poetic terms that are difficult to decipher. Most modern historians agree that the Muslims made the first assault. However, the presumption that this was carried out by cavalry is based upon romanticized images of much later Arab and Berber armies rather than the reality of 8th-century Umayyad warfare. Charles Martel then almost certainly counterattacked, following a flanking attack upon the Muslims' camp. To build upon this bald outline, the military historian is obliged to look at the lie the land, the archaeological and historical evidence for the character of this terrain in the 8th century AD, what is known about the armies involved, their elements, equipment and tactical traditions.

Given the fact that, by the mid-8th century AD, the main elements of the Muslim Army were largely mounted, at least as mounted infantry if not necessarily as cavalry, the traditional view that the Franks stood to receive an initial enemy charge still holds good. Under such circumstances Charles

Nothing remains above ground of the early medieval city of Bordeaux. In fact, one of the oldest buildings is the cathedral of Saint-André, dating from the 11th to 15th centuries, next to which is the freestanding 15th-century Tour Pey Berland bell-tower in the centre of this picture. (Author's photograph)

Martel probably occupied a defensive position ahead of Vieux-Poitiers with its flanks anchored upon dense woods and the similarly wooded valley of the Clain. One of the only two reasonably coherent accounts of the battle of Poitiers is found in a text by the so-called *Anonymous of Cordoba* who, though Christian, was writing within the Umayyad Islamic province of al-Andalus. He emphasized the solidity of the northern Christians' position, describing it as a 'glacial wall'. In this he may have been referring to their steadfast courage as well as their static defensive tactics when compared with the 'feigned retreat' and repeated charge-withdraw-charge tactics of the Visigoths and Gascons. However, many historians have dismissed the *Anonymous of Cordoba* as unreliable where tactics were concerned as well as being dubious on other counts. Another and later source which has been dismissed as a fake by many historians may, however, preserve traditional oral accounts drawn from Moroccan folk memory. It is supposedly by Sidi Osman Ben Artan and states that the Muslim Army attacked the Frankish line all along its front at the start of day, resulting in a prolonged and equal struggle. Unfortunately, Sidi Osman Ben Artan maintained that this occurred on 11 October.

One of the few other supposed facts about the battle of Poitiers is found in a text by the so-called *Continuator of Fredegar's Chronicle*. This source is widely considered to be the most reliable and may have been sponsored by a Christian participant in the battle. However, the only distinctive information that this adds is that the Christian Army attacked the Muslim camp, which is generally assumed to be a reference to a flanking movement widely believed to have been carried out by Prince Eudes. Two points support such an interpretation; firstly that at this date the Aquitainians traditionally fielded a larger number of cavalry than the Franks, and

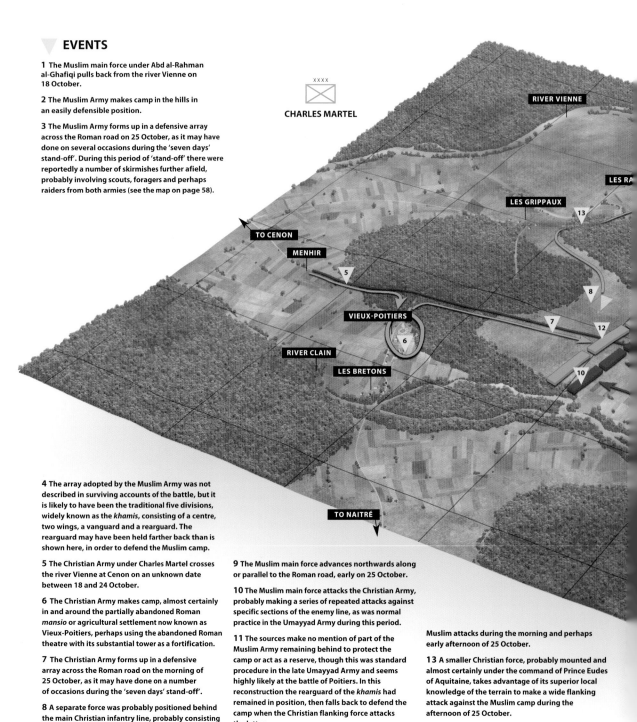

EVENTS

1 The Muslim main force under Abd al-Rahman al-Ghafiqi pulls back from the river Vienne on 18 October.

2 The Muslim Army makes camp in the hills in an easily defensible position.

3 The Muslim Army forms up in a defensive array across the Roman road on 25 October, as it may have done on several occasions during the 'seven days' stand-off'. During this period of 'stand-off' there were reportedly a number of skirmishes further afield, probably involving scouts, foragers and perhaps raiders from both armies (see the map on page 58).

XXXX

CHARLES MARTEL

RIVER VIENNE

LES RA

LES GRIPPAUX

13

TO CENON

MENHIR

5

8

VIEUX-POITIERS

7

12

6

RIVER CLAIN

10

LES BRETONS

4 The array adopted by the Muslim Army was not described in surviving accounts of the battle, but it is likely to have been the traditional five divisions, widely known as the *khamis*, consisting of a centre, two wings, a vanguard and a rearguard. The rearguard may have been held farther back than is shown here, in order to defend the Muslim camp.

TO NAITRÉ

5 The Christian Army under Charles Martel crosses the river Vienne at Cenon on an unknown date between 18 and 24 October.

6 The Christian Army makes camp, almost certainly in and around the partially abandoned Roman *mansio* or agricultural settlement now known as Vieux-Poitiers, perhaps using the abandoned Roman theatre with its substantial tower as a fortification.

7 The Christian Army forms up in a defensive array across the Roman road on the morning of 25 October, as it may have done on a number of occasions during the 'seven days' stand-off'.

8 A separate force was probably positioned behind the main Christian infantry line, probably consisting of cavalry under the command of Prince Eudes of Aquitaine, and perhaps initially stationed close to the Christian left flank to guard against a Muslim flanking attack from that direction.

9 The Muslim main force advances northwards along or parallel to the Roman road, early on 25 October.

10 The Muslim main force attacks the Christian Army, probably making a series of repeated attacks against specific sections of the enemy line, as was normal practice in the Umayyad Army during this period.

11 The sources make no mention of part of the Muslim Army remaining behind to protect the camp or act as a reserve, though this was standard procedure in the late Umayyad Army and seems highly likely at the battle of Poitiers. In this reconstruction the rearguard of the *khamis* had remained in position, then falls back to defend the camp when the Christian flanking force attacks the latter.

12 The Christian Army is drawn up in a strong defensive position, probably with both its flanks secured against densely wooded areas, resists the

Muslim attacks during the morning and perhaps early afternoon of 25 October.

13 A smaller Christian force, probably mounted and almost certainly under the command of Prince Eudes of Aquitaine, takes advantage of its superior local knowledge of the terrain to make a wide flanking attack against the Muslim camp during the afternoon of 25 October.

14 The Christian flanking attack penetrates the Muslim camp and slaughters large numbers of non-combatants, though it is unable to overrun the entire camp.

THE STAND-OFF, 18–25 OCTOBER, AND THE MUSLIM ATTACK, 25 OCTOBER

The Muslim Army retires from the Vienne and sets up camp, while Charles Martel leads his forces across the river to confront the Muslims in a series of inconclusive skirmishes

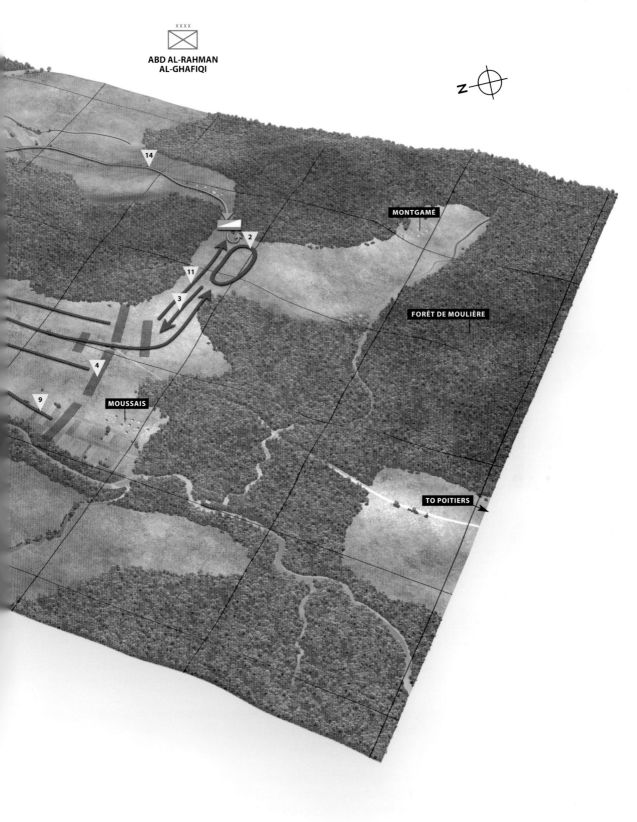

Note: Gridlines are shown at intervals of 1km/1093yds

xxxx

**ABD AL-RAHMAN
AL-GHAFIQI**

N

14

2

11

3

MONTGAMÉ

FORÊT DE MOULIÈRE

4

9

MOUSSAIS

TO POITIERS

'Sleeping Guards at the Holy Sepulchre', illustrated on a 9th-century Carolingian ivory book cover. Two men apparently wear sleeveless lamellar cuirasses of a type more normally associated with Byzantine or Islamic armies, while the third also has armour over his upper arms. (Cathedral Treasury, Nancy, France)

secondly a successful attack upon a camp, which would certainly have been to the rear of the main Muslim line, presupposes a degree of surprise and thus of superior local knowledge.

Logic as well as the sophistication of late Umayyad armies places this camp in a secure, defensible position in hills but not within a forest, while the success of the Christian flanking attack suggests that it was in some way vulnerable from another direction. A suitable location is on a hilltop, north of what was then presumably a marsh (now dammed as a pool) in a small stream flowing from a spring near the later medieval Château-de-Fou to join the Clain just upriver from Moussais-le-Bataille. Though almost surrounded by woods as well as that stream and marsh, the rear of this position was relatively exposed to fields and open pasture along the river Vienne. This avenue of approach offers the best candidate for the route taken by Prince Eudes and his presumably mounted and thus wide-sweeping flank attack. What the *Continuator of Fredegar's Chronicle* actually wrote was:

> Prince Charles boldly drew up his battle line against them and the warriors rushed in against them. With Christ's help be overturned their tents, and hastened to battle to grind them small in slaughter. The king Abdirama [Abd al-Rahman al-Ghafiqi] having been killed, he [Charles] destroyed [them], driving forth the army, he fought and he won. Thus did the victor triumph over his enemies.

The only reference to a charge is the word *inruit*, which is better translated as 'rushed in' followed by the overthrowing of the tents. However, the poetic phraseology was lifted almost word for word from the Latin translation of the Old Testament.

It is extraordinarily unlikely that the Muslim camp would have been left totally unprotected, given the professionalism of Umayyad armies and Abd al-Rahman al-Ghafiqi's previously very successful career as a military

commander. What may have happened was that the threat to, or attack upon, the camp resulted in the main Muslim force pulling back to defend its tents, booty and perhaps its families. Whether this was on al-Ghafiqi's order or was, as some have suggested, a spontaneous reaction by undisciplined Berber warriors is unknown.

Once again the dubious text attributed to Sidi Osman Ben Artan offers an admittedly unreliable explanation, with Eudes' fresh troops attacking the Muslim rearguard, which was itself perhaps defending the camp, and massacring all they found there. The North African historian Abd al-Wahid Dhanunn Taha certainly blames the Muslim defeat upon the 'unreliable Berbers' who, he maintains, were primarily concerned to protect the families that they habitually brought on campaign, and that this fact was known to Prince Eudes. Chronologically, it seems likely that the first attack upon the Muslim camp took place in the afternoon or early evening of 25 October. That this was followed by the Muslims pulling back to defend their camp, and that Charles Martel's main force advanced, not necessarily in immediate pursuit, then attacked the Muslim camp which, given Umayyad and Berber traditions, was probably protected by some sort of field fortifications.

It was almost certainly at this point, and while defending the fortified encampment, that Abd al-Rahman al-Ghafiqi was mortally wounded, either by an arrow or more likely by a javelin. Nevertheless, the Christian assault was repulsed. The dubious account by Sidi Osman Ben Artan maintained that the Muslims had not fallen back at once, having been uncertain what to do. Charles Martel supposedly took the opportunity of their hesitation to charge and , during the resulting fighting, al-Ghafiqi was hit by a javelin that penetrated a 'fault' in his armour.

We know nothing about what happened in the Muslim leadership following the fall of Abd al-Rahman al-Ghafiqi. His successor as governor of al-Andalus, Abd al-Malik Ibn Qatan al-Fihri, seems not to have been present at the battle and might have been installed as *wali* some time later. On the

GRAHAM TURNER

THE DEATH OF ABD AL-RAHMAN AL-GHAFIQI (pp. 70-71)

Following a flanking attack upon the Muslim camp, which is believed to have been made by Prince Eudes and his remaining Aquitainian forces, the Umayyad Army fell back to defend its tents, booty and camp followers. This first attack was then followed up in the late afternoon or evening by a major assault by Charles Martel's army (1). Although this was beaten off after heavy fighting, the Muslim commander, Abd al-Rahman al-Ghafiqi was killed (2), either by a javelin or an arrow. Javelin-armed cavalry were characteristic of several Western European armies of this period, including Bretons (3), Basques and Gascons. The bulk of Charles Martel's troops would, however, have fought on foot (4) though perhaps arriving on the battlefield as mounted infantry. The Christian forces probably included a relatively small number of close-combat cavalry (5). The Muslim Army similarly largely consisted of mounted infantry who nevertheless normally fought on foot, including Umayyad professional *muqatila* soldiers (6, 7 and 8), archers armed with the large, simple rather than composite Arab bows (9), and large numbers of tribal volunteers (10). Evidence from various sources, including the earliest known Arabic book of military advice by Abd al-Hamid Ibn Yahya, also describes Arab forces arranging their tents as an enclosed area, further strengthening their field fortifications (11).

other hand, this new governor was described as being one of the 'original settlers' of al-Andalus, and may well have been selected by the army before being officially recognized by the more senior governor of North Africa. Though Abd al-Malik Ibn Qatan al-Fihri may have been sent from North Africa following news of his predecessor's death in battle, the first interpretation is more likely for the simple reason that the surviving lists of Umayyad governors include those who were in place only briefly or temporarily, without chronological gaps.

THE MUSLIM RETREAT

Under the command of the new governor or otherwise, the Muslim Army used the cover of night to withdraw from the battlefield in good order. They left their camp intact, including their prisoners, a huge quantity of booty and, so it is said, many of their own non-combatants. The latter point seems highly unlikely and the unfortunates involved were probably captives from southern Aquitaine or even farther afield who might have been mistaken for 'foreigners' by the barely civilized Frankish warriors who overran the Muslim encampment the following day. Isidore of Beja, in his near-contemporary history of these events, reported that the Muslims left their tents standing when they retreated, to delay the Franks and mislead them into believing that the Muslim Army was still in position. If so, the trick was a complete success for there was no pursuit of the retreating Muslim Army during the night of 25/26 October, nor even, it seems, the following day.

Having pulled back past the formidable and still Christian-held fortifications of Poitiers, part or perhaps the bulk of the retreating army paused a short distance south of that city. A supposed grave of Muslim troops slain during the battle was believed to have been found at Moussais-le-Bataille during the 19th century. Even if it was correctly identified, the lack of archaeological information about the orientation of the bodies prohibits us from knowing whether it was a mass interment by the victors, or was done

Le Passage, the site of one of the most important fords across the river Garonne near Layrac, upriver from Agen. After defeating Prince Eudes outside the city of Bordeaux, Abd al-Rahman al-Ghafiqi's army marched up the left bank of the Garonne, sacked Agen, crossed the river then marched back along the right bank before defeating Eudes again. (Author's photograph)

The Muslims reportedly sacked a monastery or hermitage at Saint-Emilion after they defeated Prince Eudes in AD 732. It is not clear quite what existed here at the time and although the famous rock-cut church is certainly very archaic, its oldest chapel is thought to date from the late 8th century AD. (Author's photograph)

by the Muslim Army before its retreat. Other supposed 'Saracen cemeteries' were reportedly uncovered between Sainte-Maure and Nouatre north of the river Creuse, at Montgame, and on the road between Cenon and Jumeau.

Charles Martel's army drew up for battle next day, ready to attack the Muslim camp once again, only to find it abandoned by its defenders. It was, of course, promptly pillaged, the wealth found there being sufficient to stop the poor and somewhat primitive northern warriors in their tracks. Meanwhile Charles Martel was aware that other serious political and military problems awaited him along the Frankish Kingdom's Rhine frontier in Germany, though this might have been an excuse to save face because Charles' loot-laden army was now clamouring to go home.

Any Muslim units operating west of the rivers Vienne and Clain also withdrew and it has been suggested that part of al-Ghafiqi's main force fled across the Clain, perhaps cut off during the battle, though this seems unlikely.

The dating of this stone slab from the Cordova area, illustrating the story of the Prophet Daniel, is a matter of considerable debate. It is usually regarded as late Visigothic, before the Islamic conquest of the Iberian Peninsula. However, it has many similarities with secular carvings from the period of the Umayyad Caliphate of Cordoba and slightly later, while the soldiers in the lower register look more like Muslim Andalusians than Christian Visigoths. (National Museum of Archaeology, Madrid, Spain)

The Caliph Hisham's palace at Khirbat al-Mafjir in Palestine was decorated with wall paintings as well as stucco carvings. These were strongly influenced by Byzantine art and included this remarkable picture of an infantry archer with a broad-brimmed helmet, shooting at a fortification from beneath his shield. (Rockefeller Museum, Jerusalem)

Whoever these Muslims troops were, they are likely to have been pursued by any Frankish force covering the road from Poitiers to Tours via Loudun.

What we do know is that, shortly after the battle of Poitiers, Charles Martel withdrew northwards through Orléans and Auxerre. On his way he deprived the bishop of Tours of his power and expelled Bishop Eucherius of Orléans from his diocese, replacing him and the already exiled Bishop Aimar of Auxerre as rulers of these cities with Frankish counts answerable directly to Charles himself. It seems to have been left to Prince Eudes of Aquitaine to pursue the retreating Muslim forces. Amongst his most pressing tasks was to clear enemy stragglers from the area east of the river Vienne, between Tours, Poitiers and Bossay-sur-Claise. Other troops pursued the enemy via Guéret, capital of La Marche. All this evidence suggests that Eudes had either reassembled a proper army or that he had previously fled northwards from Bordeaux with more of his army intact than is generally realized.

The narrow but steep and wooded gorge of the river Boivre runs a short distance from what was, in the 8th century AD, the northern fortified walls of Poitiers. The Muslim army therefore had to march across a narrow and vulnerable area of flat land between the city and the Boivre. (Author's photograph)

In AD 732 the basilica of Saint-Hilaire-le-Grand lay outside the fortifications of Poitiers and was surrounded by its own small suburb. No attempt seems to have been made to defend the church, which was sacked and burned by the invaders. What remained of the Merovingian basilica was later completely rebuilt. (Author's photograph)

The presence of Eudes at Guéret, and information that the Muslims went past the ancient abbey here without attacking it, indicates that this part of the Muslim Army – perhaps its main element – was heading for the Rhône Valley where other Muslim forces were already involved in a separate though subordinate campaign. A perhaps legendary account recalls how a certain Saint Pardoux resisted in the supposedly fortified church of Esprit-Saint at Guéret where he and a small band of local warriors defied the passing Muslim Army.

To succeed in such a long and hazardous retreat demonstrates a remarkable degree of sophistication, communications, command and control. Yet, given what other Umayyad armies had done and were still doing in far distant parts of the world, it comes as no surprise. Having either linked up with Muslim forces in the Rhône Valley, or having reached territory under Muslim control or sufficiently cowed not to attack the retreating army, the latter made its way

The river Clain is smaller than the Vienne and is seen here at Domine, looking downstream. The battle of Poitiers was fought on 25 October AD 732, in the relatively confined area between the wooded banks of this river and the forested hills beyond, both of which formed significant barriers for the armies involved. (Author's photograph)

safely to the Muslim-ruled city of Narbonne in Septimania. Whether they were the same group that sacked the abbey of Monastier-sur-Gazielle in the Velay area south-east of Le Puy is unclear, though they might have taken this route from Guéret, via what are now Montluçon, Clermont-Ferrand and Le Puy to the Rhône and Muslim-held Nîmes.

Meanwhile, the tenuous evidence of local traditions and place names suggest that Muslim units cut off west of the river Clain made their more disorganized way home, supposedly spending at least one night camped on the wooded heights of Touche-Noiron in Deux-Sèvres and moving south along a Roman road towards Saintes. Their presence entered local legend while yet others found refuge in the heights of Neuville, Loudun, Châtillon and Champdencers. Several Aquitainian sources report that the Muslims continued to raid and devastate as they marched south, still operating as a coordinated

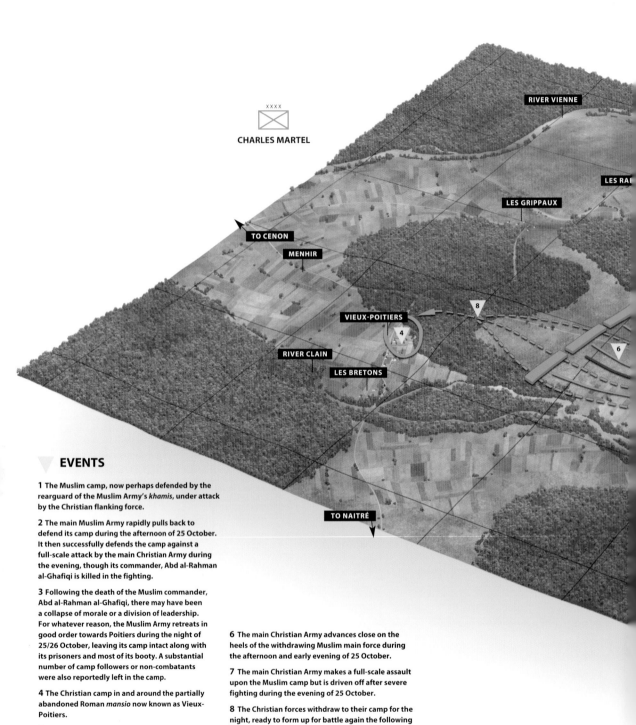

RIVER VIENNE

LES RAI

LES GRIPPAUX

XXXX

CHARLES MARTEL

TO CENON

MENHIR

VIEUX-POITIERS

4

8

6

RIVER CLAIN

LES BRETONS

TO NAITRÉ

▼ EVENTS

1 The Muslim camp, now perhaps defended by the rearguard of the Muslim Army's *khamis*, under attack by the Christian flanking force.

2 The main Muslim Army rapidly pulls back to defend its camp during the afternoon of 25 October. It then successfully defends the camp against a full-scale attack by the main Christian Army during the evening, though its commander, Abd al-Rahman al-Ghafiqi is killed in the fighting.

3 Following the death of the Muslim commander, Abd al-Rahman al-Ghafiqi, there may have been a collapse of morale or a division of leadership. For whatever reason, the Muslim Army retreats in good order towards Poitiers during the night of 25/26 October, leaving its camp intact along with its prisoners and most of its booty. A substantial number of camp followers or non-combatants were also reportedly left in the camp.

4 The Christian camp in and around the partially abandoned Roman *mansio* now known as Vieux-Poitiers.

5 The Christian flanking attacks seems to have been beaten off or to have withdrawn as the main Muslim Army returned to defend its camp.

6 The main Christian Army advances close on the heels of the withdrawing Muslim main force during the afternoon and early evening of 25 October.

7 The main Christian Army makes a full-scale assault upon the Muslim camp but is driven off after severe fighting during the evening of 25 October.

8 The Christian forces withdraw to their camp for the night, ready to form up for battle again the following morning of 26 October, only to find that the Muslim Army has retreated towards Poitiers, leaving its camp, prisoners and booty behind.

THE CHRISTIAN COUNTERATTACK AND THE MUSLIM RETREAT, 25–26 OCTOBER

Following their unsuccessful attack on the Christian position and the Aquitainian assault on their camp, the Muslims pull back to to await the inevitable Christian assault.

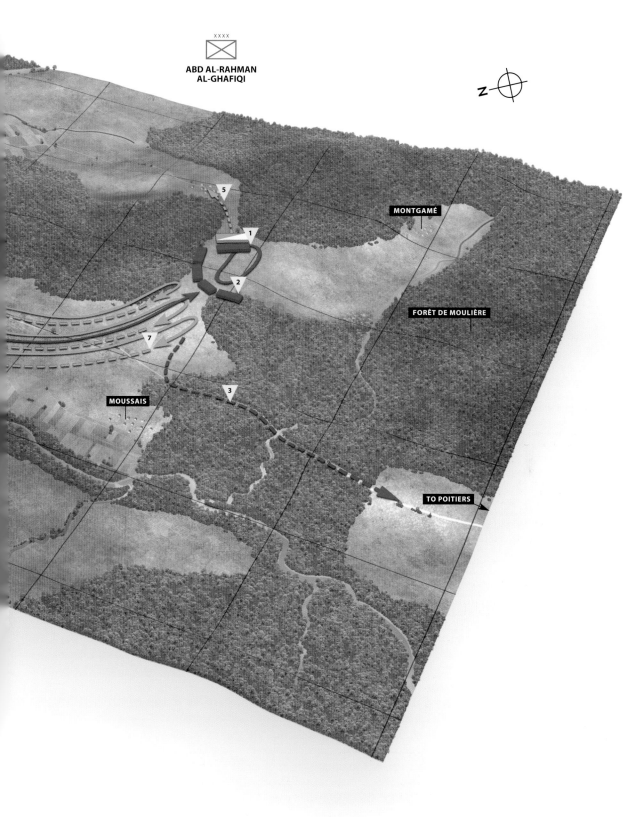

Note: Gridlines are shown at intervals of 1km/1093yds

xxxx

ABD AL-RAHMAN
AL-GHAFIQI

N

5

1

2

7

MONTGAMÉ

FORÊT DE MOULIÈRE

3

MOUSSAIS

TO POITIERS

and far from defeated army or armies. The Poitou, Limousin and, less
certainly, the Perigord, Quercy, Albigeois and Toulousain regions all suffered.

Amongst the layers of legend that overlay the battle of Poitiers in AD 732
are those concerning Muslim casualties. The earliest account by Isidore of
Beja may have been primarily based upon those of his Muslim Andalusian
neighbours. As a result the battle of Poitiers is portrayed as an indecisive
setback with relatively few losses when compared with the previous disaster
outside Toulouse, where Muslim casualties were admitted to be huge. On the
other hand, some modern scholars have attributed the reticence of Muslim
sources to the fact that the battle of Poitiers was a humiliating and best-
forgotten defeat. This naturally raises the question of the name given to either
or both of these battles in later Muslim sources; namely the *Balat al-Shuhada*
or 'Road of Martyrs'. The central significance of an ancient Roman road
at the battle of Poitiers supports the idea that this was the true 'Road of
Martyrs' and that such a name presupposed substantial casualties. On the
other hand the name may originally have been given to the catastrophe
outside Toulouse. Furthermore, the massive losses recorded in Paul the
Deacon's *History of the Lombards* – 375,000 Muslims to 1,500 Christians –
may itself have been a confusion of the two events by a chronicler writing
decades later in Italy.

The actions of the main Muslim force as it successfully retreated to
Narbonne via the Rhône Valley does not suggest that it consisted of shattered
fragments and terrified fugitives. On the other hand, those who followed a
more westerly route in an effort to retrace their original advance at the start
of the Poitiers campaign do seem to have been attacked more often and to
have suffered greater losses, especially in the mountains as they struggled
back across the Pyrenees. One unsubstantiated tradition recalled how

retreating Muslim troops sought refuge in the Bigorre region of the western Pyrenees but were defeated by local warriors led by the priest of Tarbes, Saint Missolin. In reality Missolin lived at an earlier date, though his name might well have been attached to a localized if small-scale military success. Nevertheless, it is worth noting that the new governor of al-Andalus had no difficulty in raising another army the following year.

Then there are legends that some Muslims, captive or otherwise, remained in the general area of the Poitiers campaign. The existence of 'Saracen' settler populations has been claimed in various parts of Poitou, notably along the river Vienne and between the lower Vienne and the Loire. Other evidence suggests that the Aquitainians took many prisoners during the pursuit or mopping up, mostly women and children who were then used as agricultural slaves until most were sold back to their families, as was normal practice at the time, at the slave-markets of Arles, Marseille and Narbonne. Meanwhile bands of Muslim troops continued to roam the area of Neuville, south-west of the battlefield, until they too were assimilated as 'free men' in the Deux-Sèvres region.

These stories were reinforced by the supposed uncovering of a number of 'Muslim' weapons in the region. Supposedly Islamic-style military equipment is said to be found in private collections at Des Fontaines, including daggers from Bressuire and the Thouars areas. Unfortunately these have not been published, with one possible exception. Furthermore, their identification as Islamic was made at a time when virtually nothing was known about 8th-century Islamic arms and armour, which was, quite erroneously, assumed to be similar to that of later centuries. The most that can be said with certainty is that Prince Eudes came back to a devastated land, that his alliance with Charles Martel was tenuous and that it did not outlive Prince Eudes' own death.

The Muslim forces operating in the Rhône Valley and Auvergne region in AD 732 surely cannot have been there in retaliation for the Muslim defeat near Poitiers. Not only would it have been too late in the year to launch a new campaign from Narbonne, but also the admittedly few known dates, and the efforts which the main retreating units from Poitiers made to join their colleagues, indicate that this had been a separate if subordinate campaign. It may, indeed, have originated as a diversionary raid to draw Charles Martel's attention in that direction.

While the main Christian and Muslim armies clashed in the open area between the river Clain and the wooded hills, Prince Eudes of Aquitaine is believed to have led a broad flanking movement, almost certainly by mounted troops, around the east of the hills. He then crossed these hills to attack the Muslim camp. (Author's photograph)

Their activities are even less adequately recorded than are those of Abd al-Rahman al-Ghafiqi's larger army. One group of raiders was, for example, ambushed by local landholders near 'Riom', not far from a gulley whose name recalls this event as the Ruisseau-des-Sarrasins. In fact the present town of Riom did not then exist as anything more than a village, whereas ancient Riom (Riom-le-Vieux) was clearly an important settlement. It is believed to have been located on the nearby open plain at a place now called Les Routisses where there are substantial classical ruins. Far to the north the cities of Autun and Sens were meanwhile plundered though it is unclear where this attack came from. The local Burgundian duke is also believed to have established an alliance with the Muslims in an effort to preserve his tenuous independence from the Merovingian Frankish Kingdom. He would fail and Charles Martel would ruthlessly crush Burgundian autonomy a few years later.

Finally, though not perhaps entirely unconnected in the broad sweep of Umayyad strategy, there was a Muslim maritime offensive in the western and central Mediterranean during AD 732. It included naval attacks against several still Byzantine-ruled islands; Abd al-Malik Ibn Qatan al-Fihri successfully raided Sicily while Abd Allah Ibn Ziya al-Ansari raided Sardinia. This was the first time that both islands had been attacked within one sailing season, which certainly suggests an intensification of the Umayyad naval campaign. Meanwhile there was no Byzantine response on this naval front, resistance being entirely passive. Further afield, AD 732 saw the end of a major and long-lasting Khazar Turkish offensive against the caliphate's 'central front' in the Caucasus and Armenia, which coincided with a substantial Muslim raid against the Byzantine Empire's heartland in Anatolia, in what is now Turkey. This was in turn led by Abd Allah al-Battal, the man who would become the new hero of the Arab–Greek, Muslim–Byzantine struggle in both historical fact and Arabic literary legend. His predecessor as 'epic hero' had been Maslama Ibn Abd al-Malik, brother of the Caliph Hisham, who retired in AD 732.

The land which Prince Eudes' flanking attack had to cross was steep, rugged and in most places densely covered with forest of heathland. This was presumably why Abd al-Rahman al-Ghafiqi made the fatal mistake of not anticipating an attack from this direction. (Author's photograph)

AFTERMATH

In al-Andalus the most immediate consequence of the disastrous *razzia* into France and the death of Abd al-Rahman al-Ghafiqi was the appointment of a new *wali* or governor, Abd al-Malik Ibn Qatan al-Fihri, who remained in post until AD 734. News of the disaster had, of course, been sent to the *wali* of North Africa who promptly sent reinforcements, perhaps under al-Fihri. Whether they were really ordered to avenge the defeat or simply to ensure that the Christians took no advantage remains unknown. What is known is that Abd al-Malik Ibn Qatan al-Fihri crossed the Pyrenees in AD 733, ravaging both sides of the mountains. One force is said to have marched via Pamplona and another via Gerona. Their primary purpose was to punish the *Baskans* (Basques and Gascons) who had attacked fugitives from Abd al-Rahman al-Ghafiqi's army the previous year. There was, however, no attempt to invade Aquitaine. The governor also established new and perhaps primarily military colonies along the Ebro Valley and within Basque territory. Thereafter the Muslims' main military efforts were in Catalonia, Aragon, Navarre and Septimania, strengthening those towns already in their hands.

According to the near-contemporary *Chronicle of Moissac* the subordinate governor of Narbonne, Yusuf Ibn Abd al-Rahman, lauched another raid in AD 734, which struck the lower Rhône region, temporarily taking Arles,

A number of pieces of military equipment have been dug up at Moussais-le-Bataille, some of which might date from the time of the battle of Poitiers in AD 732 and some of which clearly do not. It is, of course, quite likely that some of the dead from the Muslim army were buried here, close to the edge of the battlefield, perhaps in a mass grave. (Author's photograph)

83

Saint-Rémy-de-Provence and Avignon before pushing up the Durence Valley. Whether this Yusuf Ibn Abd al-Rahman, sometimes known in Christian sources as Athima, was the same man as Yusuf Ibn Abd al-Rahman al-Fihri who was subsequently sent from Syria to serve as governor of al-Andalus from AD 747 until 756 is unknown and, indeed, unlikely. He was certainly not the son of Abd al-Rahman al-Ghafiqi.

In AD 734, Abd al-Malik Ibn Qatan al-Fihri, was replaced as governor of al-Andalus by Uqba Ibn al-Hajjaj al-Saluli who was put in place by his patron of the Qays faction, Ubaydullah Ibn al-Habhab al-Mawsili, the powerful *wali* of both Egypt and North Africa. However, Uqba's subordinates in Tangier and southern Morocco now acted in a harsh manner towards the Berbers, triggering the revolt that had been simmering for years. Uqba Ibn Hajjaj al-Saluli himself died in AD 740, probably at the 'Battle of the Nobles' where he was in command of an Andalusian force that was practically wiped out by Berber rebels in northern Morocco.

For his part, Charles Martel had achieved much more than merely defeating a large-scale Islamic raid by his victory north of Poitiers in AD 732. Prince Eudes of Aquitaine was now his vassal while the powerful bishops of Burgundy were mere satellites of the Frankish Kingdom. But instead of taking military advantage of his new position, Charles Martel acted with moderation, forming local alliances with the Burgundians as he tried to extend Frankish control down the Rhône Valley. Only two years later in AD 734, however, the Frankish representatives were expelled from Lyon and the Burgundian 'sub-kingdom' reasserted its independence. The death of Eudes of Aquitaine early the following year, and the succession of his more assertive son Hunald, meant that Charles could not immediately punish the Burgundian 'rebellion'. Instead he launched a campaign against Prince Hunald of Aquitaine before, in autumn AD 737, he again arrested the 'unreliable' bishops of Orléans and Auxerre as a prelude to the reconquest of Burgundy. Such problems closer to home meant that the affairs of Islamic al-Andalus hardly concerned Charles Martel at all.

The impact of the Poitiers campaign on Aquitaine was much more serious, despite the Christian victory. The year AD 732 had witnessed Prince Eudes' first major defeat and had prevented him from becoming a serious rival to Charles Martel. To paraphrase the renowned medieval historian Henri Pirenne, without Abd al-Rahman crushing Eudes, Charlemagne's rise as ruler of the greater part of Western Europe would not have been possible.

Eudes had accepted his new position as Charles' vassal, but his successors Hunald I, Waifer and Hunald II did not. As a result Aquitaine would remain the Franks' bitterest enemy within what eventually became France. In fact the Aquitainians resisted repeated Frankish invasions, most of which penetrated only a short distance to plunder and besiege fortresses. Eventually, however, the much greater military potential of the Franks triumphed;

The story of the martyrdom of St Aventinus and his colleague St Gratien later became popular across medieval France. They and their fellow pilgrims are said to have been caught by 'Saracens', probably from the Muslim advance guard or vanguard which had crossed the river Creuse at Port-de-Piles, and were killed at Civray-sur-Esves. Here the story is told on a 12th-century carving on the church at Saint-Aventin, in the foothills of the Pyrenees. For reasons that are unknown, one of the Saracens is shown as a cripple – a motif found elsewhere in southern France and northern Italy. (Author's photograph)

After the battle of Poitiers the largest part of the Muslim Army withdrew eastwards, across the hills and valleys of the Auvergne towards the Rhône Valley where other Muslim raiders were also operating. Separated groups probably retreated up the valley of the river Dordogne, through Beaulieu and past the spot where the Chapelle des Penitents would be built in the 12th century. This rugged region preserves several traditional stories concerning raids by 'Saracens', though some seem to confuse Saracens, Vikings, Magyar Hungarians and even local bandits. (Author's photograph)

Hunald II was defeated and Lupus, 'prince of the Gascons' as he was known in Frankish sources, handed over his lands to Charlemagne.

The Muslim presence in Septimania was, of course, a factor in this struggle and Prince Waifer is said to have unsuccessfully attacked Narbonne, perhaps in AD 749 when a famine in al-Andalus was expected to have weakened its Muslim garrison. Eventually the Franks rather than the Aquitainians overthrew Umayyad rule in Septimania in AD 759, their success and occupation of Narbonne making Waifer feel even more vulnerable now that he was almost surrounded by hostile Frankish forces.

The long-term impact of the Poitiers campaign upon northern France, the Low Countries and Western Germany is harder to decipher. Nevertheless, this victory would eventually enable Charles Martel's Carolingian successors to dominate the entire region, attracting further support as success bred success. Before that, the death of Charles Martel in AD 741 once again fragmented the Frankish Kingdom with his eldest son Carloman becoming mayor of the palace in Austrasia, Alemannia and Thuringia, while his younger son Pepin the Short became mayor in Neustria, Burgundy and Provence. Yet this was temporary and Pepin soon emerged as the sole, if still only nominal, ruler of the Franks.

It has been suggested that Charles Martel's campaigns were conservative and defensive whereas those of Pepin became expansionist and aggressive, Pepin's wars against the Muslims in Septimania being the best known. Even so, Pepin's wars in Italy would eventually prove more important for the course of European history. What Charles Martel and the Carolingians gained from their various successes against the Muslims was huge international prestige. This they skilfully used in their dealings with the papacy, not least as an excuse to interfere in Italian affairs.

The impact of Abd al-Rahman al-Ghafiqi's defeat in AD 732 had a much more profound impact upon those northern regions of the Iberian Peninsula that were either under only nominal Umayyad authority or were already effectively independent. Here the indigenous Christian population was encouraged by the Muslim defeat and some rose in rebellion. Nevertheless the new Umayyad *wali*, Abd al-Malik, reacted swiftly with military campaigns in Catalonia, Aragon and Navarre where he subdued the lowland Basques

Charles Martel later became a heroic figure in the history of medieval France, his defeat of a substantial army of Muslim raiders at the battle of Poitiers in AD 732 evolving into an epic in which he saved European Christendom from Islamic conquest. In this copy of the *Histoire de Charles Martel*, made in France around 1470, the warriors are, of course, dressed in the armour of the later 15th century. (Bibliothèque Royale, Cod. 8, f. 42, Brussels, Belgium)

in AD 733. Farther west and south, in the Duero Valley and what is now Galicia, the superficially Muslim Berbers who had settled these regions similarly rose in revolt of AD 740 or 741. Although this was not a direct result of the Muslim defeat in Gaul, the events of AD 732 had weakened Muslim authority and undermined Arab prestige. A more immediate cause is likely to have been Berber sympathy with the current Berber revolt in North Africa. Whatever the motivation, it reportedly resulted in Andalusian Berber forces marching against Toledo, Cordoba and even Ceuta on the northern tip of Morocco, thus gravely weakening an already tenuous Islamic military hold upon what is now north-western and northern Spain. One of the leaders of the Berber revolt within the Iberian Peninsula was Kulan al-Yahudi whose name indicates that he was of Jewish Berber origin or even, perhaps, still an adherent of Judaism. He is said to have attempted to drive the Arabs from al-Andalus but, with the failure of his coup, most of the Jewish Berbers who had accompanied the Islamic conquest of the Iberian Peninsula appear to have returned to North Africa, many settling in the Temesma area.

These developments enabled King Alfonso I of Asturias to take over large areas. Despite many myths associated with this earliest phase of the so-called 'Reconquista', it is highly unlikely that these events made much difference to the indigenous population for whom it was merely a change of rulers. The 8th century AD would also see the still small Christian kingdom of Asturias making an almost total break with its pre-Islamic, Visigothic past and begin evolving into something new and strongly influenced by the emerging culture of Islamic al-Andalus.

In the Islamic Umayyad province of al-Andalus itself, the defeat of AD 732 was as yet regarded as little more than a setback. It certainly did not rate very highly in the events of this period as recorded by Arab chroniclers.

Nevertheless, the battle of Poitiers would be followed by civil conflict amongst the Muslims of al-Andalus; a conflict much like several others that took place prior to AD 732. While the frontier with the Christian north was stabilized, even if only for a few decades, there were significant military and political changes within al-Andalus. These would certainly have their impact upon events following the collapse of the Umayyad Caliphate in the Middle East in AD 750. It is, for example, possible that during the brief governorship of Abu'l-Khattar (AD 743–45) many new, and perhaps relatively high status, Umayyad troops arrived from the Middle East to crush the Berber revolts. Some of these men returned to the east or North Africa but many others settled as resident garrisons in the southern regions of the Iberian Peninsula. Their presence may have been the reason the last Umayyad caliph, Marwan II tried to escape westwards from Syria, though in the event he was caught and killed in Egypt. They would similarly have attracted a refugee Umayyad prince and virtually sole survivor of the Umayyad dynasty, Abd al-Rahman Ibn Mu'awiya, who eventually won control of al-Andalus in AD 756.

The Berber rebellion which erupted in AD 739–40 not only undermined caliphal rule and fragmented the *wilayat* or province of Ifriqiya (North Africa) but paved the way for the emergence of autonomous local dynasties. Another area that suffered the consequences of the Muslim defeat near Poitiers was the vulnerable Umayyad subordinate province of Septimania. Nevertheless, Charles Martel's siege of Narbonne in AD 737 failed, largely because Uqba Ibn al-Hajaj al-Saluli, the *wali* of al-Andalus, rapidly sent a relief army under his lieutenant Umar Ibn Khalid. It arrived by sea but found its way upriver barred by 'fortifications' – perhaps in reality field fortifications on the banks. So Umar Ibn Khalid landed his troops on neighbouring beaches and marched overland to help the governor of Narbonne, Yusuf Ibn Abd al-Rahman. Charles left some troops to contain Narbonne's garrison and led the rest against Umar, defeating the relief army in the valley of Corbières, a few kilometres south of Narbonne and near one of the ancient residences of the Visigothic king. A few years later in AD 742, the governor of Narbonne, Abd al-Rahman Ibn Alqama al-Lakhmi, felt obliged to take part in the civil war within al-Andalus, leading his troops to Cordoba where he defeated the rival 'Syrian' party. As a result real power in the outlying towns of Septimania, including Béziers, Maguelonne and Nîmes,

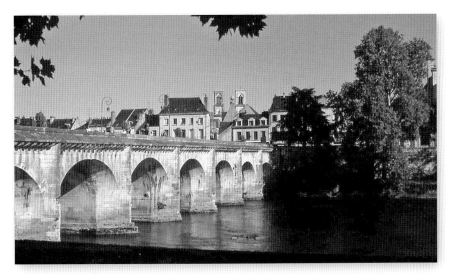

The town of Châtellerault stands on the river Vienne, downstream from its junction with the Clain but before the Creuse joins it. The town also commands a major crossing, provided with a fortified bridge in the late 16th and early 17th century but served by a strategically important ford in the 8th century AD. (Author's photograph)

'St Jerome prepares to leave for Rome', in an illustrated manuscript from the abbey of Saint-Martin, Tours, made just over a century after the abbey was the intended target of the Muslim invasion of France that culminated in the battle of Poitiers. Though highly stylized, the walls and towers surrounding St Jerome probably reflect the sort of fortifications found in central France during the 8th and 9th centuries AD. (*First Bible of Charles the Bald*, Bibliothèque Nationale, Ms. Lat. 1, Paris, France)

passed from Umayyad garrisons to the local Christian counts who enjoyed effective autonomy. In AD 750 some of them wanted to throw off Islamic rule entirely but other Christians supported the Muslims, whom they preferred to the prospect of Frankish domination.

The exact chronology is disputed, but in AD 752 Pepin the Short attacked the area and this time some local Goths led by Misemundus (or Ansemundus) rose against the Umayyads and invited the Franks into Nîmes, Maguelonne, Agde and Béziers. Helped by a Frankish force, Misemundus planned to attack Narbonne the same year but was assassinated by one of own men. Those Goths of Narbonne who feared a Frankish takeover also tried to get help from Waifer of Aquitaine. He intervened in AD 751 or 752 and in AD 757, killing many pro-Frank Goths but on this occasion the father of Saint Benoît of Aniane, the Count of Maguelonne and a friend of Misemundus, remained loyal to Pepin and responded by killing many Gascons. It is interesting to note that when the Franks took Uzès in AD 756, the *Chronique d'Uzès* described it as passing from the Visigoths to the Franks, which might support the idea that this eastern part of Septimania had never been fully under Muslim control. It is also unclear when Carcassonne fell.

Meanwhile, divisions remained amongst local Gothic counts while Narbonne held firm; the Franks being unable to take that city though they ravaged its surroundings. As the Franks had no Mediterranean fleet, it seems likely that Muslim control of the sea enabled them to retain Narbonne. This, according to the limited available evidence, largely seems to have been defended by local Christians who eventually turned upon the tiny Muslim garrison and opened their gates to Pepin the Short in AD 759. They probably did so because a relieving army, sent by the new Umayyad ruler of al-Andalus and commanded by one of his best generals, Sulayman, had been defeated in the Pyrenees, perhaps at La Unarde near Andorra. The local Goths had also been able to extract an agreement from the Franks that they would retain their own laws and privileges as they had under Islamic rule.

THE BATTLEFIELDS TODAY

The largest surviving structure at Vieux-Poitiers is the massive entrance tower of what appears to have been a small but strongly built Roman theatre. The tower, and perhaps the theatre itself, are likely to have served as strongpoints or fortifications during the 8th century AD. (Fred Nicolle photograph)

The Poitiers campaign of AD 732 ranged across regions much frequented by modern tourists. Furthermore, the routes travelled by the armies involved were almost entirely the same as those marked by modern roads, many of which follow the lines of ancient Roman roads. To study the ground of such a wide-ranging campaign it is, of course, best to travel by car, motorcycle or bicycle. With the exception of the Pyrenean passes, the generally rolling countryside is actually very suitable for a reasonably fit cyclist. Within France there are also excellent high-speed rail connections from Paris to the main cities of Bordeaux, Poitiers and Tours where self-drive or self-ride transport can be hired.

The area at the heart and culmination of this campaign – namely the battlefield and its immediate surroundings – are paradoxically visited by fewer tourists. It includes the largest local village of Cenon where a visitor is welcomed with open arms, especially if an attempt is made to speak French. The visitor will then get showered with local information pamphlets. The battlefield itself is spread over a large area and its precise locations are not always easy to find. This includes Moussais-le-Bataille, which is not a village, nor even a hamlet, but a collection of largely abandoned farms, some of which have been turned into country homes.

Two ancient tombs are said to have been found there many years ago, known as 'the King's Tomb' and 'the Duke's Tomb', but neither seems as yet to have been fully investigated. Archaeological excavations were under way at Vieux-Poitiers when the author visited several years ago but have probably now been completed. The result was a small but interesting site-museum plus, of course, the late Roman ruins themselves. It seems that the main structure was a theatre, but with other habitations, farmsteads and industrial buildings nearby.

Only a few kilometres north of Moussais and Cenon, the closest city is Châtellerault, an industrial town that has sometimes been unfairly described as one of the ugliest in central France. In fact its historical centre is interesting, and also contains the 16th-century family home of the philosopher Descartes (of 'I think, therefore I am' fame). The town itself had been a centre of iron working since the 13th century, making steel blades since the 18th and becoming one of France's main centres of armaments manufacture from the 19th century until 1968. It is now better known for its police college.

Farther south the larger city of Poitiers is a lively university town and is a major centre of French medieval studies. In addition to its most famous monuments, it has a fascinating medieval centre. Nevertheless, these buildings

Next to the remains of the Roman theatre at Vieux-Poitiers, here being excavated by archaeologists, lay a Roman *mansio* or large agricultural estate. Beyond the line of trees in this photograph lies the river Clain and a hamlet known as Les Bretons, perhaps recalling one of the many settlements of British refugees fleeing the Anglo-Saxon conquest of what became England. (Author's photograph)

East of a small wooded hill which lies behind the hamlet of Moussais-le-Bataille the open farmland rises towards the other wooded hills. It was probably here, in the open ground, that the armies of Abd al-Rahman al-Ghafiqi and Charles Martel manoeuvred during the battle of Poitiers on 25 October AD 732. (Author's photograph).

all date from well after the 8th century AD. The church of Saint-Hilaire, which stood outside medieval Poitiers, is now within its southern suburbs. It often tends to be closed so a visitor is advised to attend a religious service rather than turning up as a tourist. It also says a great deal for the French refusal to be burdened with their own glorious history, that the other biggest tourist attraction in this region is the Futuroscope. This, as its name implies, is a huge entertainment complex dedicated to the latest and anticipated future technologies, located midway between Poitiers and Moussais-le-Bataille.

The city of Bordeaux has suffered a great deal from its turbulent history, with its centre almost entirely dating from the 19th century and very few medieval buildings surviving other than the cathedral and a church or two. Nevertheless the city is full of character, excellent shops, cafes and, of course,

Another view of the main battlefield, looking north-eastwards from Moussais-le-Bataille. The wooded banks of the river Clain lie on the left and the Christian camp at Vieux-Poitiers would be beyond the distant wooded area in the centre while the Muslim camp was probably to the right of this photograph. (Author's photograph)

outlets for the superb wines of this region. Some historians have suggested that Eudes was defeated in AD 732 near a ford over the river Garonne near Agen, but this seems unlikely unless there were more clashes than the existing texts record. On the other hand this part of the Garonne plain was the scene of important strategic manoeuvering. Battlefield tourists who are enthusiastic enough to make the detour should, nevertheless, be warned about the huge numbers of summer insects – biting, stinging and otherwise – which are characteristic of the banks of the slow-moving Garonne, not to mention the lakes and ponds that dot this part of south-western France.

Dax, in the northern foothills of the western Pyrenees, is still famous for hot mineral springs dating from Roman times if not earlier. They flow constantly at a natural temperature of 64 degrees centigrade. Many people, especially the elderly, still come to take the waters and seem to spend the rest of their time playing boules next to the remains of Dax's Roman walls.

There is no problem finding all classes of accommodation in any part of France, but within the Poitiers area there are only a few registered campsites because this is not a major tourist region. One is located outside Poitiers itself and there are several along the rivers Clain and Vienne. The closest to the main battlefield are those at Saint-Cyr, one of which is very up market while the other is very simple, and also at Châtellerault, which could be described as mid-range. A few other campsites can be found along the route taken by Charles Martel to Tours and from there southwards. In contrast, there are abundant campsites around Tours itself and along the Loire Valley. A particularly pleasant, shaded, clean and inexpensive example is located at Luyon, slightly downriver from Tours.

Three registered campsites are listed in the area of the city of Bordeaux, a few are also located along the route taken by the main Muslim Army from Bordeaux to Poitiers. On the other hand there are many more on or near the coast. Similarly there are numerous good campsites in the foothills of the Pyrenees and in the area of Gascony that Abd al-Rahman al-Ghafiqi's army devastated, but there are again fewer along the route northwards to Bordeaux. Once again, there are significantly more on or close to the coast, which is a major holiday destination. Small local hotels, inns or bed-and-breakfasts are concentrated in essentially the same areas as the campsites.

Poitiers and the Poitou region lie in the southern part of what the French call the 'Garden of France', which itself stretches along both sides of the river Loire. Poitou largely consists of a pleasant, broad and sometimes dramatic landscape of uplands and deep valleys, but without mountains. It is famous for cattle, goats and being a region dedicated to food and the enjoyment of life. Wild fowl or game from the forest, as well as fish from the numerous rivers, all contribute to a distinctive and exciting local cuisine. Even a hardened battlefield tourist should try the local 'Chicken Poitevin' and the nougatine of Poitiers, which is a local form of confectionary. Then there is a local vegetable pâté that is particularly good for picnics, plus the apples of this region of orchards.

With the exception of the Landes area between the Pyrenées-Atlantiques and Gironde-Bordeaux regions, virtually the entire campaign of AD 732 took place within what are now significant wine-growing regions. Not all produce 'fine wine', though several do, while several produce remarkably satisfying 'country wines'. Even Poitou boasts a VDQS (one step below an Appellation Controlée) wine, the Haut Poitou, which is crisp, light and suitable for drinking with fish dishes. Meanwhile, the area south, east and north of Bordeaux remains the best wine-producing area in the world (unless you prefer Burgundy) and Entre-Deux-Mers, lying between the rivers Garonne and Dordogne is a massive if recently overextended region of vineyards. In fact the most likely sites of Eudes' two main defeats by al-Ghafiqi lie in what are now vineyards, unless they took place on the flat river-silt lands alongside one of these rivers. Wine tasting in at least one of the local chateaux remains a must for any non-teetotal visitor! The foothills and the area slightly north of the western Pyrenees has long produced wine but its quality and reputation has been on the rise. It is also blessed with France's greatest variety of indigenous wine grapes.

FURTHER READING

Abun-Nasr, J. M., *A History of the Maghrib in the Islamic Period* (Cambridge, 1987)

Bachrach, B. S., 'Charles Martel, Mounted Shock Combat, the Stirrup and Feudalism', *Studies in Medieval and Renaissance History*, 7 (1970) 49–75

Bachrach, B. S., 'Military Organization in Aquitaine under the Early Carolingians' Speculum, 49 (1974) 1–33

Bachrach, B. S., *Merovingian Military Organization 481–751* (Minneapolis, 1972)

Blade, J. F., 'Eudes, duc d'Aquitaine', *Annales du Midi*, (1892)

Blankinship, K., *The End of the Jihad State* (1994)

Bousquet, G. H., 'Quelques Remarques Critiques et Sociologiques sur la Conquête Arabe et les Théories émises à ce sujet', in *Studi Orientalistici in Onore di Giorgio Levi della Vida*, vol. I (Rome, 1956) 52–60

Busseau, L-F., 'Une confrontation Européenne Nord-Sud; La bataille de Poitiers de 732', *Histoire Médiévale*, 57 (September 2004) 30–37

Caille, J., 'Narbonne sous l'occupation musulmane (première moitié du VIIIe siècle): Problèmes de Topographie', *Annales du Midi*, 82 (1979) 97–103

Codera, F., 'La dominacion arabiga en la Frontera Superior y en la Galia meridional, anos 711 a 815,' *Journal des Savants* (1912)

Codera, F., 'Manusa y el Duque Eudori, Estudios criticis de historia arabe-española', *Colleccion de los estudios arabes*, 7 (Saragossa, 1903) 140–169

Codera, F., 'Narbona, Gerona y Barcelona bajo la dominacion musulmana', *Estudios criticis de historia arabe-española*, 8 (Saragossa, 1903)

Collins, R., *The Arab Conquest of Spain 710–797* (London, 1989)

Crone, P., *Slaves on Horses* (Cambridge, 1980)

Fouracre, P., *The Age of Charles Martel* (London, 2000)

Freeman, E. A., *Western Europe in the Eighth century and Onward* (London, 1904)

Fries, N., *Das Heereswesen der Araber zur Zeit der Omaijaden nach Tabari* (Tübingen 1921)

Gabrieli, F., *Il Califfato di Hisham* (Alexandria, 1935)

Gateau, A., (tr. & ed.), *Conquête de l'Afrique du Nord et de l'Espagne* (Algiers, 1947)

Glick, T. F., *Islamic and Christian Spain in the Early Middle Ages* (Princeton, 1979)

Hildesheimer, E., *L'activité militaire des clercs à l'époque franque* (Paris, 1936)

Kennedy, H., *The Armies of the Caliphs: Military and Society in the Early Islamic State* (London, 2001)

Lammens, H., *Etudes sur le Siècle des Omayyades* (Beirut, 1930)

Lecointre, Comte, 'La bataille de Poitiers entre Charles-Martel et les Sarrasins', *Bulletin de la Société des Antiquaires de l'Ouest*, (3 ser.) & (1924) 632–42

Levillain, L., & Samaran, C., 'Sur le Lieu et la date de la Bataille dite de Poitiers de 732', *Bibliothèque de l'Ecole des Chartres*, 99 (1938) 243–67

Lévi-Provençal, E., *Histoire de l'Espagne Musulmane* (4 vols) (Paris, 1950–67)

Lot, F., 'Études sur la Bataille de Poitiers de 732', in F. Lot, *Recueil des Travaux Historiques de Ferdinand Lot*, Tome II (Paris, 1970) 243–267

Maurice Bedel, 'La Bataille du Vieux-Poitiers', *Le Glaneur Chatelleraudais*, 39 (Oct–Nov 1939)

Mercier, E., 'La Bataille de Poitiers et les vraies causes du recul de l'invasion Arabe', *Revue Historique*, 7 (1878) 1–13

Mercier, M., and Seguin, A., 'La bataille de Poitiers, optiques interne et externe à l'Europe', *Revue Africaine*, 87 (1943) 33–92

Mercier, M., and Seguin, A., *Charles Martel et la Bataille de Poitiers* (Paris, 1944)

Molinie, A., and Zotenberg, H., 'Invasions des Sarazins dans le Languedoc d'après les historiens musulmans', in Devic & Vaissete (eds.), *Histoire générale du Languedoc*, vol. 2 (Toulouse, 1875) 549–58

Norris, H. T., *The Berbers in Arabic Literature* (London, 1982)

Périn P., 'L'archéologie funéraire, reflète-t-elle fidèlement la composition et l'évolution de l'armement Mérovingien?' in A. Bos (et al eds.), *Materiam Superabat Opus: Hommage à Alain Erlande-Brandenburg* (Paris, 2006) 95–111

Quiroga, J. L., and Lovelle, M. R., 'La Invasión Arabe y el Inicio de la 'Reconquista' en el Noreste de la Península Ibérica (9-251/711-865)', in D. A. Agius and I. R. Netton (eds.), *Across the Mediterranean Frontiers: Trade, Politics and Religion, 650–1450* (Turnhout, 1997) 61–86

Rouche, M., 'Les Aquitains, ont-ils trahi avant la bataille de Poitiers? Un éclairage 'événemential' sur de mentalités', *Le Moyen Age*, 74 (1968) 5–26

Rouche, M., *L'Aquitaine des Wisigoths aux Arabes; 418-781: Naissance d'une région* (Paris, 1979)

Roy, J-H., and Deviosse, J., *La Bataille de Poitiers, Octobre 733* (Paris, 1966)

Senac, P., *Musulmans et Sarrasins dans le sud de la Gaule du VIIIe au XIe siecle* (Paris, 1980)

Sherwani, H. K., 'Incursions of the Muslims into France from the beginnings up to their expulsion from Narbonne and Languedoc in 759 AD', *Islamic Culture*, 4 (1930) 110–13, 251–73 and 397–422, 588–624; 5 (1931) 71–112, 472–95 and 651–76

Slousch, N., 'L'Empire des Berghouata et les origines des Bilad es-Siba', *Revue du Monde Musulman*, 10 (1910) 394–400

Taha, Abd al-Wahid Dhanunn, *The Muslim Conquest and Settlement of North Africa and Spain* (London, 1989)

Terrasse, H., 'L'Espagne Musulmane et l'héritage Wisigothique', in *Etudes d'Orientalisme dédiées à la Mémoire de Levi-Provençal* (Paris, 1962) 757–66

Verbruggen, J. F., 'L'art militaire dans l'empire Carolingien (714–1000)', *Revue Belge d'Histoire Militaire*, 23 (1979–80) 289–310 and 393–412.

Voisin, A-R., *La Bataille de Ballan-Miré, dite bataille de Poitiers 732* (Paris, 2000)

Watson, W. E., 'The Battle of Tours-Poitiers revisited', *Providence: Studies in Western Civilization*, 2 (1993)

INDEX